Praise for THE SONG OF INCREASE

"Jacqueline's sensitive and perceptive nature is reflected through her life with bees. She encourages readers to venture further into the new multidimensional territory of honeybees. This book calls attention to the hidden aspects of apiculture and the deeper nature of bees, encouraging us to open our hearts and minds to the bees. This is a timely book in a transitional time for bees and the entire biosphere."

~ Michael Thiele, *Gaia Bees*, biodynamic apiarian,
author, educator, and bee sanctuary creator

"The Song of Increase opens up a mystical realm of deep communication with nature. Learn the wisdom of the bees, and you will never look at the world the same way again."

~ Starhawk, Author of *The Fifth Sacred Thing*

"I have been deeply moved by this book. Jacqueline's work with bees is truly extraordinary. This book has the potential to transform beekeeping and transform the world."

~ Susan Chernak McElroy
Author of *Animals as Teachers and Healers*

"This book is a treasure of honey bee philosophy. Jacqueline profiles the many ways bees connect within the hive, with the world outside the hive, with agriculture, and with the beekeeper. Spend time watching your hives. What the bees say in this book is right."

~ Nathan Rausch, biodynamic beekeeper
Snoqualmie Valley Beekeepers

Return items to **any** Swindon Library by closing
time on or before the date stamped. Only books
and Audio Books can be renewed - phone your
library or visit our website,
www.swindon.gov.uk/libraries

WITHDRAWN
From Swindon
Borough Libraries

Copying recordings is illegal. All recorded items
are hired entirely at hirer's own risk

West Swindon
Library
Tel: 465555

 **SWINDON**
BOROUGH COUNCIL

The Song of Increase: Returning to our Sacred Partnership with Honeybees

Library of Congress: 2014921269
ISBN: 978-1-942479-00-0 soft cover
ISBN: 978-1-942479-01-7 hard cover
ISBN: 978-1-942479-02-4 e-book
1. beekeeping 2. apiculture 3. spirituality 4. sustainable agriculture

Illustrations & cover design by Jacqueline Freeman
Inspired by photographs from Robin Wise
Back cover photo of Jacqueline by Robin Wise

Printed in the U.S.A.

Friendly Haven Rise Press
Battle Ground, WA
www.FriendlyHaven.com/books

"One becomes a better beekeeper by letting a bee be a bee. If everything is done in service to that, the Life Force of the colony grows and the hive thrives. How can we give bees an environment that allows them to have the ultimate and most advantageous experience of living in harmony with all their purposes?

When we satisfy that question, we will have returned to our sacred partnership with honeybees."

~ Jacqueline Freeman

DEDICATION

To Joseph, for his ongoing love, belief and support of all my ventures. I thank God every day for bringing us to this marriage and partnering you and me in this sovereign life. Bless you, my beloved husband.

TABLE OF CONTENTS

FOREWORD

I met Jacqueline Freeman several years ago when I attended her workshop on the spiritual life of the honeybee. My only experience with bees up to that point in my life was a sting on the ear from a honeybee when I was six years old. I swelled up like the Michelin Tire Man and kept a healthy distance from bees after that. But on a chance whim — or perhaps in answer to the dream whisper of that little bee from so long ago — I signed up for Jacqueline's bee workshop.

It was no ordinary class, and Jacqueline is no ordinary beekeeper.

Jacqueline was teaching the class with fellow beekeeper Michael Thiele, both members of a small and growing cadre of bee enthusiasts who practice an entirely new kind of beekeeping. Called bee-centric, natural beekeeping or bee guardianship, these revolutionary beekeeping methods emphasize the needs of the bee over the keeper's desire for honey production.

The high point of the class came when we stood before the entrance of a large and active honeybee hive. We were directed to open our arms and send the bees kindness and goodwill. Within seconds, bees poured from the door of the hive, circling us in gentle humming spirals. I stood silent and fearless and ecstatic in a swirl of bees that circled my body and all our bodies with curiosity and aerial grace. Their hypnotic, thrumming song vibrated deep in my chest long after the bees had departed back to the privacy of their hive.

When I opened my eyes, I saw that I was not the only one with tears streaming down my face. From that day, I have loved bees. I love them with a child's delight and with a mother's fierce desire to protect her family. The bees are our family. We are bound to them, and they to us through the grand and terrible process of domestication. They are part of our history and our lives, and our dependence on them is far greater now than their dependence on us. We are tied to them by necessity, for our food survival. The tie that binds them to us is immense generosity.

Jacqueline Freeman is a biodynamic farmer, beekeeper, and artist. She is also a gifted intuitive, as the women in her family line have been for generations. Jacqueline has been receiving messages and images from bees for several years now, and what the bees have told her is being revealed — bit by tiny bit — in scientific studies on the quantum nature of bees, their medicine, their communication, and their organizational structure as a superorganism. This is pretty heady stuff, and unconventional to the point of baffling at times, but what Jacqueline has experienced with her bees feels true to me down to my very bones.

This book is a compilation of information from the bees themselves and from Jacqueline's experience with her many hives. I must tell you, this book is full of the word "love." Love is, I'll admit, an often overused word. Should you doubt that this word is the least bit excessive in her use of it, I can assure you it is not. Jacqueline is a woman who lives and breathes this word into each and every relationship on her enchanted farm of bees, blossoms, cows, goats, cats, dog, fish, and chickens.

I know this because I have spent many days and nights there while putting this book together. She is ceaselessly attentive and loving to whatever creature — plant or animal — crosses her path. In the evenings, I find her gathering up lost bees into screen-topped jars, offering them a dab of honey and a familiar piece of honeycomb to rest on for the night. Writing halts for a moment when her cat Remy requests her attention which she readily shares. Weeding the garden, she'll stop to sort cow and goat leafy treats from compostable weeds and twigs. When the borage plant falls over in the heat, she sends me running for a stake and tie to keep it lifted to the sun. Each evening before bed, she and Joseph bless each animal and their farm.

This is a woman whose words I can believe when she shares the bees' message of unity, of food made with prayer and work done with great love. The bees chose the right medium for their message. Jacqueline — who she is and how she lives — is an inspiration to me. She is a woman of confidence, integrity, and great joy, and life meets her there in that place and magic and enchantment unfold around her. This web of goodness she weaves catches up all who share her world, from the smallest plant to the most peripheral of associates. She is most assuredly a woman who walks the talk of Unity.

Since that time I was enfolded in the spiral of bees, I've taken many beekeeping classes from Jacqueline and from guest teachers she brings to her farm. Jacqueline and her fellow bee-keepers are sparking a revolution in beekeeping around the world, and if the honeybee is to be saved, it is Jacqueline and folks like her that will show us how it will be done.

Sitting near the entrances of my three beehives now, I re-play the words, images and wisdom in these pages over and over again. This is not a book to read once and set aside. Keep it on your night table when you need to know that there are forces in nature working diligently and tenderly on your behalf. Reading this precious and enthralling book has made me a more hope-filled person (and a far better friend) to my bees. My wish is that you, too, may be blessed with simple grace of bees as you sit with their words and Jacqueline's.

~ Susan Chernak McElroy
Camas, Washington

INTRODUCTION

When the bees speak, I listen.

Strange as it may sound, I do hear bees talk. In my first few years with bees, questions and novel ideas about bees arose and organized themselves in my thoughts, and I found them interesting and useful. Had this continued, I certainly would have imagined myself in good connection with the bees. Then one day, in a moment of reverie, I suddenly got some eye-opening information about the role bees have in the world and a whole new understanding of bees emerged. What they had to say encouraged me to make fundamental changes in how I care for my bees.

You can label this clairvoyance, higher intelligence, deeper connection with Nature, animal communication, or the ravings of a wild bee fanatic. All I know is that I'm a better friend to bees because of what they've taught me.

FIRST BEES

When our first two hives arrived on the farm in early summer 2004, I had no experience with bees. While I liked the idea of bees I thought of them as another farm animal, one who gave honey instead of milk or eggs. A friend offered us bees and it seemed natural to accept, like we did when we were given our first chickens. We knew no beekeepers, and I hadn't yet attended a bee class but I quickly became fascinated by them. Like most people, I was quite fearful about getting stung so I bought a protective bee suit with hat, veil, jacket, pants, and gloves. Standing adrenaline-filled a good distance away from the hive, I was surprised the bees didn't fly out in a cartoon tornado to attack.

Each day I suited up to go look at my bees. I wore a long-sleeve shirt and jeans underneath the bee suit so I had a double layer of protection. I pulled on my knee-high farm boots and duct-taped the bee pants inside the boots so no bees could burrow inside. I taped the edge of my elbow length gloves over the long sleeves of the jacket. I put on my bee hat and zipped the bottom of the veil to the bee suit. I even taped the zipper in case a bee tried to get in that tiny opening. Dressed, taped, and zippered, I walked out to see the bees.

I looked like a space man suited up to walk on the moon. I put a chair next to the hives and watched. It was already hot outside, and inside the bee suit it was even hotter. Fueled by curiosity, I sat in the sun and watched the bees going in and out of the hive. I watched until my clothing was wet with sweat and the heat unbearable. I did this for several weeks.

Summer progressed and the days got hotter. I sat next to the hive in my protective gear. The bees paid no attention to me whatsoever. I spent hours next to the entrance inches from where they landed and took off and never once did a bee do anything aggressive toward me. Occasionally one would land on me in the way a bee lands on a branch or blade of grass, with no concern of me at all. The first time I didn't duct tape my pants to my boots or my gloves to my bee jacket was a big day. I felt truly adventurous. As usual, the bees didn't even notice me.

July sweltered on. Still wearing a double layer of clothing and knee-high boots, I thought perhaps I might get by with my long-sleeve shirt and jeans instead of the extra layer of the protective suit. I bravely attired myself with the hat, veil, and gloves and, brave soul that I was becoming, sneakers. Still, the bees had no response to me even though I had my nose a foot away from their landing area. I began to notice when I sat with the bees, despite the discomfort of the heat, that I felt relaxed, curious, and happy in a caring way.

I began to think maybe the reason the bees didn't try to chase me off was that I was calm around them and they were mirroring how I was, or maybe I was mirroring how they were. This was a revelation because if this were so, it meant the bees were also paying attention to me and who I was around the hive. As long as I embodied kindness around them, they treated me with the same. I questioned my original fear.

Could it be that we were connected? This idea seemed revolutionary because it would mean my bees were more than mere insects. It would mean they were capable of gauging whether I was a threat to them, and they could decide if they should trust me.

I want you to know that I didn't just one day tear off my bee suit and go hang out with bees. I was still too nervous to do that. It took years for me to build up my courage to work with them like I do now, without protective veil and gloves. That came, but in good time.

Eventually, I retired my bee suit. I realized the bees could tell what emotional or energetic state I was in and, if they found me calm, they responded by trusting I would do them no harm. The first time I walked right up to the hives wearing a T-shirt and shorts, I felt a little anxious and self-absorbed, but then I remembered to turn my thoughts away from myself, to open to them and let them feel me out — which they did. They landed on my bare arms and licked my skin for the salt and minerals. When I held a finger aside the entrance, a sweet little bee delicately walked onto my fingertip and faced me. She looked right into my eyes and, for the first time, we saw each other. Elated, I stepped into a new relationship with bees.

And so I became part of bee life.

I found myself having more intuition about the hives. One morning in early spring before the bloom, I suddenly had the idea that I should go check one of my hives. Sure enough, I found them unexpectedly out of food so I fed them honey saved from the year before. That call I intuited from the hive likely saved its life. Another time I had the feeling that a distant hive in the east pasture was on the verge of swarming. When I walked up to see, they sure enough were. Events like this taught me to trust my intuition more, which continues to bring me into a closer relationship with all the hives.

In my sixth year with bees, something new happened. Without intending to ask about honeybees, I had begun a morning practice of contemplation, quieting my mind and opening my heart. I entered this prayerful state asking for guidance, direction, courage, and truth. Even though I didn't mention honeybees, they immediately began appearing in my thoughts and passing me information I had never read or learned from other sources.

I believe the sincerity of my questions opened a door. When the information began coming to me, I listened with attentiveness, respect and gratitude — a good place to start any relationship. The more I listened, the more information they shared.

Since that time, I have had numerous conversations with the bees — plain as day. They've communicated to me in words, ideas, and images. Sometimes what they tell me is so far beyond my own intellectual base, I have to stretch to understand their meaning.

I have had plenty of opportunity to share these new ideas with bee folks. Years ago I began teaching monthly classes at our farm and coming to the aid of wild swarms. I speak at regional and national conferences, and I appeared as the swarm rescuer in the documentary movie "Queen of the Sun." As an adjunct to the film, I was invited to write a chapter for the "Queen of the Sun" book alongside people I admire like Vandana Shiva, Raj Patel, Gunther Hauk, Michael Pollan, and Michael Thiele.

Still I didn't know how to explain where the information

I was sharing came from, and that bothered me. I told my husband's friend, Steve Hall, that saying it just pops into my head sounds strange even if it is true. Steve is a holistic M.D. with a broad knowledge of many different sciences. Without a moment's hesitation he told me about numerous times in science when revolutionary ideas emerged through similarly curious and intuitive channels. While not common, information that arrives in this way has a solid history of leaping scientific thought forward.

The German chemist Friedrich Kekule dreamed he saw a snake seize its own tail. Upon waking he connected this image to a problem he'd been working on and finally identified the elusive ring-shape of the benzene molecule. Linus Pauling published the first paper identifying DNA as housed in the shape of intertwined helixes, information that came in a flash of inspiration. Pauling's ideas so often came to him this way that he set aside daily time to listen for the knowledge. Pauling received two Nobel prizes for his discoveries. Nikola Tesla, a brilliant scientist with numerous inventions to his credit, openly stated that many of his ideas, including inventing alternating electrical current, originated from such a place.

In a similar way, the bee teachings enter me.

For the most part, the information comes to me fully formed, like reading out of a book, and for that reason I call them readings. Occasionally I see images or feel an emotional tone, but mostly I hear full sentences. Sometimes complete essays came forth needing little more than punctuation.

During certain readings I've felt distinct emotional and physical responses such as when they described the quickening during the Queen's elation-filled marital flight, the debilitating feeling of sugar in a bee's belly and the shared jubilation of swarming bees. In each of these experiences, the feeling gave more depth and color to my understanding.

The hardest part of writing this book was organizing it because the bees shared information as they felt I could understand it. They often gave me a broad overview first, then explained the underpinnings and details. Sometimes I asked for the answer to a specific question, but they always told me what I needed to know first and, when my understanding was sufficient, they shared what I asked about. Once I asked in three consecutive readings by what name they call the worker bees, and I thought they ignored my question, but when they finally answered I realized I had needed to understand how they experience sound before I could rightly hear the word that represents them.

THE HIVE IS A HOLY PLACE

And that is how I enter into working with them, as if I am entering a holy place. I begin by asking that I come to their presence with reverence, respect, gratitude, and generosity. Caring for the bees who share our farm has shown me this is how they behave toward each other. I hope I have the strength of character to be like this with them and in the greater world.

Most people believe the role of the honeybee is to pollinate crops and make honey for humans to eat. Many of the bees kept by humans are pigeonholed into those two roles and often treated like indentured servants whose mission is to serve our needs. Conventional beekeeping is human-centric, designed to make it easier for people to keep bees using methods that pressure bees to produce more product for us.

Our present attitudes and beekeeping routines have strayed from bee-centric methods and are the root of the problems bees are having these days. These conventional techniques may serve marketing purposes, but they aren't always bee-friendly and compromises are often at the expense of the bees. This narrow thinking has led us to create ways of employing honeybees that keep us blind to the tremendous depth of knowledge they embody and the generosity with which they carry forth each day to serve the highest needs of our spiritual development and the evolution of the world.

Surely that is a broad statement, one that may require a second look at how we share this planet with other life as well. That's the effect a bee-centric perspective has had upon me, and I am grateful to the bees for bringing that into my consciousness. If we look at bees from the perspective of a bee (bee-centric), we become capable of asking what bees most want and how to care for them in ways that put the needs of the bees first. To do so requires an understanding of bees who live with little or no human intervention. If we know what bees do on their own and why they do that, we may be able to provide a similar environment they will flourish in.

Treating bees with reverence and gratitude will do more to help bees than you imagine. As you read about the many profound ways that honeybees offer their work to propel humankind's spiritual evolution, I expect you will be inspired by their respectful industry and fellowship. They are living examples of love, of an interdependent community, and of an ever-outflowing story of creation filled with patience, kindness, and compassion.

The book is structured so you can learn about the true nature of bees, understand bee behavior and develop a consciousness that enriches your interactions and appreciation of them. I've included many personal anecdotes about bees in the hope these stories explain the way I interact with them and our ongoing bee-human relationship. Each chapter in this book concludes with a section that is in the words of the bees as they were revealed to me.

In all respects this book has been co-written. People have asked who it is I believe I am speaking with during these communications, so I will offer you my experience: The relationship I have with bees isn't with any one hive or single bee. Most of the communication seems to come from a consciousness — an Over-lighting Bee — that oversees the work of the bees and is capable of explaining the purposeful actions of the bee kingdom. I've done my best to convey what they've taught me.

So you get all of us in this book — me with my humble human education augmenting the brilliance of the bees. Unlike most beekeeping books, this book is not about methods, treatments or systems. Instead, our way is one of kind observation, creating supportive homes and fields for bees to live in, and tending the heartfelt relationships we create by being together. My hope is that your relationship with bees as a keeper, a gardener or simply a caring friend to bees, becomes gloriously rewarding for you and the bees.

As my husband is fond of saying when he hears these stories, "They have the ring of truth to them." I invite you to listen for that ring of truth as I share these insights from the bees. What I've learned at their wings is the most profound education.

~ Jacqueline Freeman

THE SONG
OF
INCREASE

RETURNING TO OUR SACRED
PARTNERSHIP WITH HONEYBEES

THE SONG
OF
INCREASE

1

Song of Unity

Honeybees call themselves a "Unity." The Unity includes the bees and all their surroundings. As part of their world, we, too, are part of their oneness. When the bees speak about embracing us into the Unity — a theme they return to often — I think of the many times I've sat beside my hives and been privy to exactly that. Being with bees is an experience hard to put into words. The who and what of the honeybee remains an enigma and a paradox: The honeybee is both an individual being, and a cell in a larger being.

They are — if you can imagine this — both particle and wave in the physics of their world.

My dear friend and fellow beekeeper Michael Thiele writes, "When we step into the world of Apis Mellifera, we are entering a multidimensional landscape of being. The life gesture of the honeybees is so unique and different from most other life forms that a rational mind alone cannot provide sufficient understanding of its nature. Although they are one of the most studied animals, questions about their lives remain. Rudolf Steiner described the bees in his lectures as a 'world-enigma.' It points towards an understanding that goes beyond reason, and it is an invitation into another mode of awareness."

We begin our journey into the world of the honeybees by exploring their largest self first: the colony and its environs. From this vision of their wholeness, we can first glimpse the elusive, mysterious wonder of Unity. The honeybee is an exemplar of unity consciousness. They seem to have worked out all the kinks inherent in living for the collective.

In Our Own Words

We wake up to the understanding that we are all one, all the time. Mankind exists connected each-to-each but believes that they are not. Honeybees dwell in the full realization of that connection and have done so for eons. The unity we embody is a reflection of the kingdom-wide unity that dwells in us all.

This is the gift we bring: complete, sacred Unity in body and spirit. To be in the presence of spirit, to simply sit and "be" in such presence, can offer the opportunity to be transformed by it. This, we offer you. Come sit. Be with us. Drink in the Unity as you would fresh rain. We offer our gift with great joy and love!

THE BIEN

"In the Presence of Spirit"

Bees live in wholeness. They dedicate themselves to work within the hive in a way we humans don't grasp because we have individual personalities. Bees don't have personalities; they have the hive, and each individual pours love into the care and keeping of their colony. Daily, they live teachings we could benefit from learning.

Each member of the hive community dedicates 100 percent effort to all interactions. That's quite an interesting idea to me because I was raised with the idea that 50-50 is the goal for a two-person relationship. For larger groups, each giving a little bit carries a group forward. The hive model of 100 percent effort given to all tasks by every bee is a wild idea that got me thinking, what if we set aside our indomitable nature and put the betterment of all in front? What would that do to our relationships, communities and the whole world?

Intrigued by such a brave and generous commitment, my husband and I decided to give this crazy idea a try. We've been married a few decades, and as all couples do, we have devoted plenty of time into solidifying what causes us upset. An example would be who does the dishes. While we aren't tit-for-tat every time, if one of us does dishes three times in a row, it certainly would be brought up as reason for not having to do dishes that fourth time.

Being willing to do everything the marriage requires 100 percent of the time is a tall order but we tried it anyway. While we don't pretend perfection reigns in our marriage, we are pleased with how this idea has changed our behavior. Giving 100 percent has instilled a sense of order we hadn't expected. If I do dishes six times in a row — without complaint — chances are my husband has also already stepped up to doing more of the things I don't relish, like making dump runs or keeping our vehicle tanks topped off so I don't get my hands dirty pumping gas. Truthfully, I don't mind doing dishes much anyway and he doesn't mind digging deep holes to plant trees, something for which I lack talent.

Every bee has total commitment to doing whatever the colony requires. When a need comes up, the task is answered without hesitation. I've seen a bee signal to another "I've got an itch I can't reach," "the floor is sticky," or "I dropped a pollen pellet," and other bees jump in to help. While working inside the hive, I inadvertently broke a honeycomb which fell on the hive floor and made a mess. A whole posse of bees quickly started licking up the honey and carrying it off to store. No one said, "I'm busy." Everyone jumped in and cleaned up the mess, then went back to their other tasks. I could tell by their hum there was no blame, frustration or anxiety, just easy going cooperation. Each bee does what needs to be done to move the colony forward. How utterly divine that they put the colony first.

Imagine if we did that, if each day we put our best self forward and did whatever it was our community — local or world — required to keep the world going in a way that supports all life. Could we be so brave and generous? I don't know the answer to that on a large scale, but I do know that living in a relationship where the needs of the marriage come before my and his personal needs gives us both a more harmonious and rewarding marriage.

Being in Unity with myself and all that surrounds me, at first surprised me. I was used to having personal territory that I assumed needed protecting. Coming from a place of unity is curiously different. I feel both supported and unfolded. This keeps our marriage focused on true partnership.

Sitting next to a hive, watching bees flying in and out, my mind clears of conscious thought as I enter a deep state of "bee meditation." Many bee stewards, I'm sure, know this state. We sit next to the hive and, as the sound of the hive enters us, we find ourselves in a deep reverie that opens our hearts. The bees draw us into this opening heart and welcome us there. It is a heart filled with great love and great activity.

A typical bee colony is made up of thirty to fifty-thousand honeybees living inside a magical womb-like enclosure. Though individuals, every bee within the colony works for the good of the hive to help it function perfectly. Honeybees are interdependent and rely upon each other to create the working hive that allows and encourages them to flourish.

Science describes honeybees as a superorganism. The hive is a single entity made up of tens of thousands of individuals cooperatively working together and functioning as one living being. Each area of the hive and the tasks of all the bees depend upon each other for full expression.

A word that has a more enhanced meaning is the German word for the hive community, the "Bien." Besides the qualities of the superorganism, the Bien also includes the spiritual center and life force of the hive. Collectively the Bien is conscious and alive, like a living brain, and operates as a unified thought.

The Bien encompasses, too, a relationship to place, light, seasons, and plants. The Bien is not just the hive, but this hive in this particular and sacred place. Bees are creatures of home and place and grounding.

Within this holy landscape of the Bien, bees work with flowers, trees, minerals, water, light — the full spectrum of Creation — to bring about the highest good for our earthly environment in ways we'll explore in upcoming chapters. Unknown to most, bees also work intimately with the unseen realms of nature spirits, elementals, and faeries. All actions are both for the singular unit of their Bien and also for the Unity of all Biens everywhere.

A single honeybee alone can't perform the many necessary survival tasks a bee needs; nor can a honeybee survive without its hive. If a foraging bee gets lost or trapped during its travel and is stuck somewhere overnight, most likely she will be dead by morning. I believe her death comes from the separation.

Bees understand they do not exist solitary though they each have individual roles. Rather than saying they act in unison, like a group that works toward a common goal (which they do), they reference a larger perception of awareness. They are beings who carry memory and meaning through time. While each bee lives a short life, the hive itself continues on into time. This is key to understanding their use of the word "memorist," which was new to me as well.

Bees progress through a chronological sequence of tasks over their lifetime. Old bees die as new bees step forward to fill the prior bee's role. They take on the tasks with a fully expressed presence that expands into the history and future of each bee. The consecutive line of bees continues into time, and the hive functions as a perpetual presence. Like a hologram, the hive carries the wholeness of its expression through time. Each hive is continually populated by bees on into eternity. Although individual bees die, the Unity or Bien, is capable of living forever. In their world beyond the hive walls, bees bring life, song and spirit to all they touch, making their larger community a more vibrant, abundant place.

We humans have tasks and are aware of our personal history, but most of us feel somewhat disconnected from the history of our human world. We know stories from the past, but we don't readily embody the lessons and knowledge of our history, and we certainly don't grasp our future. Some humans, like indigenous aborigine and pygmy tribes, hold the tribe's memory and indeed even its future awareness in their ken. They are connected in a way that most of us have forgotten.

Sitting quietly beside a beehive — or sitting quietly in any natural setting — is one simple way of finding our way back to such a connection. When we quiet our minds we reveal ourselves, our goodness. When we embrace our place within the wholeness of our landscape and our community, we open to our larger, better selves.

During reflective moments with my bees, I hear something indefinably enriching and fulfilling in the hive's sound, this "single tone made up of thousands," and I am bettered by it.

Imagine if we woke each day asking ourselves how could we better the world? How could we sing ourselves into aliveness? Who would we be if we understood we are all connected, that our individual efforts have great value when we undertake actions that better the world whole?

JACQUELINE FREEMAN

In Our Own Words

A hive is a wholeness. One bee experiences all that each bee experiences. There is no separation.

Where you have separation, we are born into a world beyond the borders of singularity. Our first thought is always of the hive, to bear increase in the world as we sing the world into aliveness. Bees in a Unity of purpose have the fortitude and attention to meet each task with a steadiness of spirit. Each does the task at hand, does what needs to be done to carry the hive into its fullness of being.

We are not soloists, though we each make our own sound. We are memorists who have remarkably retentive memories. We come to the hive, and we are the hive. We sing our Unity, then each take our song out into the world. We touch each flower and deliver the signature of our creation. After our touch, each plant has a rising helix, a chromatic cord that joins earth, matter and ether. The fecundity of the atmosphere is thus enhanced and enlivened.

Pollination is much more than fertilization. The act of pollinating moves reproductive forces and, at the same time, enlivens the ether. Pollinating and the daily revitalizing of the ether is our task. We are embedded into the task as it is in us, and we have no singularity of it.

Bees and humans are different in our forms, yet we are unified in our mission of spiritual evolution. We bring knowledge of these spiritual forces that you may know how love and generosity of spirit create the world anew each day.

Where the song of the hive is strong, the nature spirits flourish. The hive is a beacon of light where work and love go hand in hand. To the nature spirits, each hive and each bee is wrapped in light. The sound of an industrious hive is so full of life that it feeds the soul. Hives are sources of spiritual nourishment for the nature spirit kingdom and places of deep reverence. Nature spirits come here and recharge and rejuvenate themselves, filling themselves with spirit. The hive light is living food, living nourishment. Hives are like shrines, places that generate great amounts of healing, loving and creative energy. Bees and their hives are shrines — temples of the spirit world, source points of spiritual manna.

Humans have an individual soul. The hive and all hives have a group soul. Animals have a group soul individualized. Bees have a group soul intact, never separate. Each bee is part of a fully experiencing group soul. We live and breathe in Spirit always, fully connected. In this evolution of the group soul, every hive, has consciousness of every other hive. We unify in a harmonic, all sounds finding a commonality, a single tone made up of thousands.

Show yourself to us that we may embrace you into our Unity.

COLLAPSING COLONIES

"Losing Our Center"

No doubt you have heard of the problems honeybees are having. Bees by the millions are abandoning their hives, and tens of thousands of bees are falling dead in cities and across farms and fields. All over the world, honeybees are vanishing. No single cause has been attributed to this catastrophic decline. Some blame it on mites, viruses, and/or genetic alteration of crops. Current research heavily implicates a particular brand of pesticides called neonicotinoids. Likely it is many overlapping causes. When a friend of mine contracted cancer at a young age, her oncologist told her it was the result of "a thousand little insults, over and over again, to the body and spirit." This may be the story of colony collapse as well.

When I spoke with the bees about colony collapse, what the bees told me captures in a nutshell a host of the topics we will open more deeply in the chapters to come. Specifically, the bees spoke about relationship. Everything the bees do is about relationship with one another. The story of colony collapse is a story of how these relationships have been broken, contaminated, or subverted. It is a story of ignorance, thoughtlessness and selfishness — qualities we humans bring to far too many of our relationships, from the most personal and intimate, to the most global and institutional.

In the chapters to come, you will hear much about the complexities and the subtleties of relationship, because right relationship truly is at the heart of Unity consciousness, which is the heart and soul of the Bien. But this particular story concerns one specific and critical relationship to bee health and survival: the relationship of bees to pollen.

The bees say colony collapse begins with pollen. This sounds like a simple response, but it is not. Bees have a deep, complex and ethereal relationship with plant pollen and require a multitude of pollen types to keep the colony in good health. With spray-poisoned, gene-manipulated pollen and with only minimal varieties of pollen available in our vast swaths of monoculture, suddenly the door is open to the "thousands of little insults to the body and spirit."

Nature has a mission to bring to the future through the offspring, each life form and its genetics. If the life form is weak, the reproductive process is shut down so deficient genetics don't carry forward into the future. To do otherwise wouldn't make any sense and would weaken the line. Current statistics cite 15 percent of couples in the U.S. as infertile. It looks like a lot of honeybee Queens are also missing the life force required to be viable mothers of future bees. In the U.S., the medical response has not been to strengthen infertile couples; instead it's been to find more clever ways to trick human bodies into becoming pregnant. Hence we have fertility drugs and multiple egg implantations leading to octo- births. This misses the point completely, which is to fix the problem at its source and create HEALTHY beings (humans and bees) who can easily carry new babies and their lovely perfect genetics forward. Sadly this approach seems to lack enough profit to benefit the medical establishments.

The solution for bees is found in treatment-free beekeeping, appropriate food (honey, not sugar), clean forage (more power to us that we can keep educating and encouraging that), and to get away from the conventional factory farming methods of raising bees. That is a big checklist, but we have to start somewhere if we expect bees to survive in our human-tainted world.

I hope I don't sound defeatist here. I do believe each of us has to become politically active and educate everyone we can. We either make the earth cleaner or dirtier. Let's not make bees suffer as a result.

The Overlighting Being

While the hive itself is conscious of each undertaking, and the purpose and means of completing each task, we fret when these projects are not accomplished. The colony is aware of its strengths and weaknesses and works to surmount its insufficiencies. As such, the energetic tone of the hive may fluctuate.

A hive seeks to address its shortcomings. The colony desires that which makes them whole. We try to remedy our problems and many hives do, but some hives are not able to survive. Though they have Life Force, and they work to fulfill the tasks of a colony, these bees cannot fill the directive to thrive because they are broken. Hives populated with these wounded bees are markers, given the task to evolve or devolve when exposed to things like pollen with an altered gene structure or nectar that can damage organs.

Each bee aligns itself with cosmic forces that direct its role in the colony. These paths are inestimably clear and all of us are tuned in. The daily functioning of the hive is precise and rhythmic, each bee's task divinely orchestrated to fulfill the role of the hive.

Collected pollen emits a sound vibration that fits neatly into the historic memory bees share. When pollen is chemically altered, the atomic structure has a strange vibration that doesn't fit what we know as common to our perception and knowledge.

A hive can accommodate some insufficiency within the pollen's vibratory expression because there is enough volume to make up for a bit of weakness. That's okay because the wide variety of sources provides ample stores for the hive. But if only one kind of pollen is made available to us, as is done in monoculture cropping where bees are trucked to pollinate thousands of acres of only one kind of flower, we cannot gather the wide variety of necessary herbal, tree, and flower pollens we use to regulate our immune systems and fight off disease.

As we collect and bring home the pollen, the vibration of the pollen tunes us to a channel that bees work within. Clear pure pollen, rich with Life Force, directs us in the proper action and relationships with all that surrounds us. Our sensitive antennae are tuned to a channel that gives us the ability to communicate with other bees as well as to stay connected to Source. The more vital the pollen, the more it dials us in. Each bee knows its task and purpose via the constant communication that comes through the clear channels of the antennae.

The clarity of our actions is determined by the strength of the channel and the purity of the pollen. When pollen is nutritionally weak, it doesn't provide sufficient energy to the hive to make it thrive. When only one pollen is available, bees sicken. Pollen is absolutely primary. Pollen is the determinant of the hive's health. When pollen is molecularly altered by exposure to poisons, the poison damages the genetic material and its vibratory expression.

THE SONG OF INCREASE

All damage has an effect.

We feed pollen to our young larvae, the pips, and the food they ingest calibrates the dial-in that connects bees with their purpose. When pollen is damaged, the dial-in is not quite as accurate. So while the next generation of bees may be functional, they are not optimal. The pollen fermentation process, wherein the chemical structure can be aligned to a degree, can handle minor discrepancies, but when there is too much alteration, fermentation can't fix it.

When a bee is born its antennae are attuned to the channel of the bee's highest expression. When a young bee has had insufficient nutrition and inadequate vibration from the pollen, the bee suffers. Its channel isn't tuned in clearly. It lives with a modicum of static that distracts and inhibits the bee's access to full knowledge and expression.

Each hive has an Overlighting Being. The Overlighting Being is the representative of the hive and at the same time has the responsibility to the bee kingdom. The Being ensures that each hive is aligned with the highest expression of its bee-ness and contributes to the bee kingdom's evolution. The Overlighting Being is the repository of the hive's history and the emissary who speaks on their behalf. When the bees bring in pollen, the Overlighting Being revels in remembrance and appreciation of each plant's genetic materials and vibratory expression.

A hive exposed to and altered by impaired pollen bears a dispiriting hollowness within the sound expression of the hive, which affects all levels of the hive. While a hive can carry that condition for a while, ultimately the lack becomes predominant and the hive is aware that it is coming up short. This static-like sound continually distracts and draws energy from the tasks at hand and inhibits the singular focus of the bees.

39

Humankind remains unaware of how significant its alterations are to chemical structures, how detrimental these alterations are to finely tuned channels of expression, such as bees. Poison alters the environment on so many levels.

When toxic exposure to living beings is gauged, the results are only measured in human scale; what Man cannot measure is deemed insignificant or unknown, and thus allowable. Even when damage is acknowledged, it may be permitted nonetheless. No weight is given to how genetic aberrations damage the vibration and inhibit the Life Force of bees.

When a hive's attunement to purpose is thwarted by exposure to chemicals, molecular disorder, genetic disruption, or atomic disarray, the effects are heinous and devastating. When a hive loses its signal clarity and gets skewed, the hive becomes unable to find its center. The richness of sound that invests the core of the hive is diffused and dispersed; its connection to purpose is obscured and ultimately lost. At this point, the Overlighting Being, acting in correct relationship with Nature, invites the hive to remove itself from the bee family.

The hive recognizes that it can't stay tuned in to its evolutionary purpose, so the colony removes itself. They sacrifice themselves so their weakness doesn't carry forward.

Without migratory beekeeping, Man cannot have monoculture. Monocultures are a betrayal of the trust between bees and Mankind. Though there will be protest, this false movement of bees must cease. Monoculture is too hard on hives.

Each hive must have the autonomy of serving its own needs and being in service to the larger purpose. The ability for autonomous thought is our protection. Decisions made for bees without our input put us at risk. Man in his folly has taken over making decisions for the health of bees that do not serve us in our ongo-

ing evolution. We have desire to work with man, but not to be enslaved.

If migratory beekeeping and toxic misuse of our lands continue, all will be lost with some pockets of survival if these pockets are not over-managed. Misrepresentations of our intentions need to be removed. The virgin queen in her mating needs choice of what drones she mates with and the hive needs to decide on its own how to make the hive strong.

Let our natural practices express through our own tastes and timing. We ask that Man enter with us into a revolution of agricultural practices where together we seek respectful relationship with all beings.

THE SONG
OF
INCREASE

11

"The Song of Belonging"

Within the great breadth of the Bien dwell the small bees, like cells in a brain — or thoughts in a vast mind. Each individual bee has an important role in the successful function of the hive, and we humans have given them names that evoke certain roles in the human community, such as "queens" or "workers." We name the male bee by his sound: "drone." But these names minimize the life and work of the honeybee. A queen is not so much a hive monarch as the hive mother. The word worker implies a small tone of drudgery. Drone hints at a sound no one wants to hear, as in "droning on and on..."

Yet, within the hive body and out in the fields, the individual bees go about their tasks with astonishing focus, devotion and energy. The Queen pours herself into her work as mother to every bee in the hive. She has no task other than to serve. Other than ask for a drop of food, she does nothing on her own behalf. The workers — I call them maidens — take up many "professions" in their short life and do them all with gusto and joy. I know this from speaking with the bees, but any perceptive beekeeper feels the sense of delight and enthusiasm at the door of most hives.

In conventional beekeeping, drones are thought good only for impregnating Queens. With the hive's Queen already pregnant, drones are commonly labeled useless disease vectors and a waste of resources within the hive. Yet bees call drones "the holiest of beings" who function much as holy shamans within their own and neighboring hives!

Maidens, drones and Queen work together in a cooperative culture that celebrates joy, calling and beauty. Those of us privileged to gaze within the inner workings of a successful hive see a world of sensuous, amber-colored beauty. The combs in naturally kept hives undulate in exquisite organic patterns. The scent wafting up and out of a hive is intoxicating — a mixture of nectar, resins, and the glandular aroma of the bees.

All this industry and beauty is created by an insect no bigger than a fingernail, living in a perfected communion most of us have lost long ago in the ancestral reaches of our time. The bees help jog our memories of what it is to live a life of devotion, joy, and loving membership in a strong, committed tribe.

In the following chapters, we will explore the individual lives of the bees and let them tell us about their unique and inspiring culture.

THE SONG OF INCREASE

We are the measure
Wing to tip, hand to hand,
All the drones, cell by cell,
As throat of flower
To length of tongue.
As time before love's last forage.
Track of sun our distance dance
As egg to pip to cycling ray
As seasons go, the comb now filled
As Queen's round heel, forever ever.
*   ~ The Bees*

THE MAIDENS

"Messengers of Light"

As you can tell, I spend many an hour sitting near my hives watching them come and go. I revel in the enveloping sound, and I thoroughly enjoy the innocence of wondering what they are doing. These hours are mind-freeing, heart-expanding times when I am single focused in my heart with nothing extraneous: no stress, complication or worry. Just simple time with the bees.

One day I saw a drone land at the entrance and begin to wiggle to and fro in place, signaling some kind of upset or concern. I wondered if the wiggly drone might be looking for a "cleaner" bee. When something is not quite right with a bee, like an unreachable itchy spot, that bee will squirm around and even brush up against other bees, telling everyone that something is tickling, biting or bothering and asking for help to remedy that.

The role of the "guard" bees is to defend the front door and prevent bees who don't live there (including wasps and yellow jackets) from coming in. This task also means making sure pests or diseases don't make it past the entryway. The drone was calling for a cleaner bee to help get the itchy thing off him before he went inside.

A moment after the wiggly signal, a maiden dashed over and gave him a thorough cleaning. She climbed on top and scoured his back, reached under his wing surfaces and the wing joint. As she examined his abdomen, she found something and bit it, then jumped aside and spat it out. I couldn't tell what it was (though I suspect a mite) because she lunged on it and bit it again, then another bee jumped at it and the little speck fell off the edge. The cleaner bee stepped aside and the drone walked calmly inside.

For every task of the hive, there's a maiden ready to do it. Author Gunther Hauk, in his book *Toward Saving the Honeybee*, describes the maidens this way:

"Truly, the term 'labor of love' would apply to the workers, whose selfless activity is a source of marvel and amazement. The concept of 'love' is not used here in the way Hollywood presents it...but rather in its true meaning, namely that 'love' is work; work utilizing and applying wisdom, insight, understanding."

Ah, the maidens, the sweet, sweet maidens. Most of the activity in the hive is done by the maidens. Indeed they comprise 90 percent or more of the hive's year-round population and nearly 100 percent in winter. The maidens are models of harmony, integrity and devotion to the hive.

To make a hive fully functional the maidens cooperatively undertake a vast variety of tasks. After 21 days in a honeycomb cell, a maiden bee is born. She chews her way out of the cell and turns nearly at once to assist the nurse bees by cleaning and tending the brood cells in the nursery. A few days later, she becomes a nurse bee who feeds the pips her glandular secretions of royal jelly. A tiny bit of royal jelly protects the larvae from bacterial infections, and in more quantity is also the steady diet of any queen cells in gestation.

Each task is done in sequence as the maidens mature. They build comb, feed and care for the Queen, maintain a communication network, inoculate new bees with intestinal flora and feed everyone in the hive. They maintain an ideal temperature year round and bring in water as needed. They gather, process and store nectar and pollen. They keep the hive air healthy, regularly clean out dead bees and clean up live bees and the hive. They defend the hive from intruders, seek out nectar and pollen sources and carry everything back to the hive. They create propolis and use it to seal the hive. They prepare for swarming and when necessary, find a new home. If the Queen dies, a maiden may step in and lay eggs (more on this later). If any one of these tasks is found wanting, the hive suffers. If all are done well, the hive thrives.

The maidens are the backbone of the hive and nearly all tasks fall to them. In busy summer months, the life expectancy of a maiden bee is about 45 days. They work themselves to the full expenditure of their capacity and die with tattered wings, after thousands of trips to tens of thousands of flowers. So strong is their devotion to the hive that, if separated from their family overnight, they may perish of loneliness.

In Our Own Words

We are the Messengers of Light. Our tasks are more than the work at hand. Though we may look small, each fills our role and thus bee, hive, kingdom, all phyla and the world move forward together.

JACQUELINE FREEMAN

We ask you to bear this knowledge that you may know our shared evolution:

Little bee with a thousand eyes,
Tall human with two,
The rising sun pours into us.
The light fills us with awe
Bare naked we fear ourselves alone.
Robed in awareness, we know each matters.
Each is cousin to the other.
Illuminate with these words.
Hear our song. Know our task.
Share our joy, as each day breaks
We create the world again.

Evolution isn't random. We all work together. The act of working together IS the evolution. Cooperation between us accelerates development of each species. The way we hold and support ourselves and each other advances our shared evolution.

Everyone has a voice, from the littlest to the biggest. Some know and hear the voice of ALL THAT LIVES, others say that can't be true because it shakes the foundation of their faith.

We beings of light ask you to know we are all connected. Would you ignore that and choose to believe some are separate, some are dominant? We are embodied in the knowledge of our connection. Some of you believe you stand alone. In our beautiful connected world, nothing stands alone. There is consciousness in everything. This is God's voice and how God speaks to us.

NAMING THE MAIDENS

Usually when I speak with the bees I simply listen to what they've chosen as the day's lesson. A few times I've asked a question and hoped they would address it. Sometimes they answer directly; other times they speak about something that seems unrelated. So it was when I first asked about the maidens.

My friend and fellow beekeeper, Michael Thiele, found it hard to believe that the bees would call the hive's females "worker bees" as humans have named them, and he wondered how the colony refers to them. Though the females do much of the colony's tangible work, Michael thought it disrespectful to call them by their job titles and wondered if they were acknowledged with a more comprehensive name that describes them as more than their tasks.

I asked the bees what they called the females. They responded by telling me about their consciousness. I assumed they were ignoring me so I asked again the next day. They told me how they perceive the vibration of sound. I waited a few days, and they didn't mention it so I didn't ask again. Then they told me.

Upon hearing the answer from the bees, I realized they explained the answer to me on the first day, but I needed some groundwork before I would be able to make sense of the answer, which didn't come until the third lesson.

The first lesson told me more about the interior of the hive, the safety of the area where they begin their lives. The second lesson described the tasks they learn as they move from one function to the next. During the third lesson, below, they generated a sequential developing sound much like a Tibetan chant. It began focused on the interior, then transformed to an open expansive tone that reverberated out into the whole world. Like an OM in reverse, they said. The opposite of we humans, who first are external to our own perceptions, then grow and progress to knowing our interior world. Along with this deep explanation, they also gave me a short answer: maidens.

In Our Own Words

The Arc of Creation opens with a blessing, a sound that names us. We dwell in the enclosed area, the interior of the hive, for the first part of our lives. The interior space is a safe enclosure filled with industry. When we mature, we move outdoors to the larger world. Our name is the interior space that comports us to the exterior, all while in a shared space of consciousness.

Humans wake up in an external world and you work your way to learn of the interior. You first know the external world, the open sound of OM. As you progress in your development, you come to know your interior world and the sound moves into you.

Thus OM begins with the sound of all the world and then carries you inside to the sound of one.

We come into the vast interior world embodied in service, and then we go out into the land-world with our gift. Our name begins in the enclosed space of the hive in the surrounding humm-mmm, in and through all of us. When we transition outside to foraging, our sound opens to the wide world. Though the image infers time moves from one to the other, our name tells this all at once. To you, our name sounds like the chant of OM sung in reverse.

THE DRONES

"The Holiest of Beings"

The first time I saw a drone up close, I marveled at his enormous eyes, so large they covered his entire head. "Surely," I thought, "there is something more to see when one has eyes that big." No stinger either. They are not made for war. They are made for love.

Often I have lain in the grass with a drone or two on my hand, watching them walk up and down my fingers, in no hurry at all. They seem to be happy wherever they are and within their own contemplative rhythm. Unlike the maiden bees who scurry to get their tasks completed, drones wander slowly, with tempered curiosity and composure, at one with the world.

Drones (male bees) make up a small part of the hive's population, about 10-15 percent in the foraging seasons. In conventional beekeeping, drones are presumed needed for one thing only: mating with a virgin queen.

In conventional beekeeping, Queens are artificially bred and not impregnated in the wild. Most beekeepers believe drones simply take up space, eating honey that could be better used by the maiden bees or harvested by the beekeeper. Due to their size and longer gestational cycles, drones may also be magnets for parasitic insects that target the drones while they are still larvae. Following these beliefs about the lack of usefulness of the drones, most conventional and even some natural beekeepers cull and kill the drone eggs, leaving only maidens and a Queen.

Interestingly enough, no matter how many times beekeepers find and kill the drones, the Queen continues to lay more drone brood to replace the missing ones. Beekeepers think they're helping the hive by freeing it of drones, but the hive obviously doesn't feel that way. The hive wants drones. Drones carry the genetic line of their hive's Queen. As long as drones from this hive mate with virgin queens from another hive, the hive's genetic line continues.

The drones do see more with their enormous eyes. Bees experience their hive as a Unity of shared thought, so when the drones fly out, the hive's Queen and the maidens experience the world through the drone's heightened sensitivity. Because a hive shares consciousness, when a drone flies out to breed or to visit other hives, all the bees of his hive visit as well. Through their drones, the colony perceives the inner chambers of other hives — the sights, sounds, scents, and emotions — and is connected to the wisdom and knowledge of the greater bee community. In this way a drone has a freedom that expands his hive's experience and knowledge.

Drones look different from female bees. They have enormous eyes, a large stinger-less body, and a more leisurely pace than the maiden bees. Rudolf Steiner called drones "the sense organ of the hive" and said they are responsible for communicating to the hive the feeling states in which the hive dwells.

The bees told me drones are "the holiest of beings," and are exquisitely conscious of the sense impressions within the hive. The drones are also fully in connection with the historical context within which all bees dwell. They transmit this knowledge to the unborn bees through the drone's magnificent song. Drones sing of the bees' role in the world and, through their song, convey bee culture to the next generation of bees.

When the holy drones sing to the babies, I imagine them much like people of aboriginal and African cultures who sing ceremonial songs that birth the babies into life. These tribal people believe the birth song the babies hear welcomes them into this world and conveys important knowledge to the babies, telling them where they have come from in the past and how they and their tribe move into the future. These tribes believe that people who are born without hearing their birth song struggle through their lives because they are untethered and don't comprehend where and how they fit in the world.

The drone song tells the new bees about the journey of the bees through history from the ancient past to the present, and from here how the bee kingdom moves forward into their future. Their song describes the spiritual and functional purpose of honeybees.

While the drones sing their ancestral song, the babies are also surrounded by a second song sung by the maidens: the hive's song. This vibratory lullaby permeates the eggs in their cells and speaks to them about life within the hive in the present moment.

Bees need to know the individual tasks they will take up in and out of the hive. They also have to know their larger purpose — the role of the bees within the world. The hum of the maidens tells the bees what they will do once they are born. The song of the drones tells them why they will do that.

The drones are the only bees who sing the song that instills in the new bees all their ancestral knowledge. The babies are thus born with an inherent knowing within them. If new bees don't hear the drone song and don't learn this language, bees are less able to fulfill their role in the fields and on earth.

Within the hive, drones are present to convey to the hive's future foragers the intelligence they will carry out to the fields and bring to the flowers. In a robustly healthy hive, each bee resonates with the drone song. Inside the hive the drones bring forth the balanced sound vigorous hives make — the sound of healthy, exuberantly alive hives.

There is another clue that hints at the unique role the drones play; unlike maiden bees, drones are able to visit other hives. Each hive has its own distinct scent that comes from the Queen's pheromone. All bees in that hive carry her scent on them. If a maiden bee from one hive goes a-wandering to inspect the pantry of the hive down the lane, the second hive's guard bees know immediately by her scent that she is not from their hive and they'll chase her off to prevent her from robbing them.

Maiden bees in a strong hive sometimes try to enter other hives to find out if they can steal the other hive's honey and enlarge their own larders. These "robber" bees test the second hive's guard bees to see how secure their front door is. If it's weak, they'll gather up an invading force to steal the other hive's honey. For this reason, all guard bees defend their entrances and don't allow intruders from other hives inside.

But drones can visit any hive. They land at the entrance, stroll past the guard bees, and head inside. The guard bees step aside and let them enter even though they know the drones are from another hive.

Why would the guard bees do that and where are the drones going? Common sense would say that the first place you wouldn't want strangers to go in your home would be the nursery where all the babies are, but that's exactly where the drones go. The drones head directly into the brood chamber where the developing pips are. They join other drones in two tasks, providing warmth to the brood and singing the drone song.

The drones maintain the song of the world. They hold and create the prayer that carries the hive along. If a hive were a ship, drones would be the keel. They are at the center of the healthy functioning of the hive.

In Our Own Words

The drones sacrifice themselves. They are the holiest of beings. They make the prayer sound within the hive and are not distracted by tasks. They sing and their sound fills us with love. They make a round sound that surrounds us with prayer. They sing for the babies, sing for the birth. Their sound pulls the babies as they are being born, through the light of creation and imprints the unborn bees with the vibration of creation. The song, the Arc of Creation, moves through the hive like a prayer, becoming part of the vibratory being of each bee. As the bees mature, they come to embody information that is later passed on to the flowers during pollination.

The Creation Song is knowledge. The song tells about a world with the sky and the earth and a horizon between. Drones sing their song to template the birth door. During gestation they encode each larvae with the knowledge of 'how to bee' overlaid with cosmic knowledge that blueprints how the world comes into being each day and how the hive helps carry the world into the future. When the larvae are sufficiently mature, the Creation Song calls them out of the cell and stimulates the sensory organs of the baby bee. The linkup is an invitation and an answer, a call and response as they leave the cell.

The sound the babies have been immersed in describes an imagination of a hexagon even as they are being formed inside one. This image, as they grow, will come to have great meaning to them. Within the Creation Song is an elaborately precise vibrational communication about the organization of minerals, and a map of the relationship of the mineral forces contained in pollen. This chemical language reveals the right relationship between the minerals, with a specific awareness of silica.

While the drones sing, the baby bees are also imbued with a sense impression of the practical tasks of the maidens through the constant hum and vibration of each task within the hive. The movement of the comb and the progress of individual tasks occurring upon it are vibrationally conveyed to all bees in the hive. From the maidens, the babies hear and understand the industry of the maidens in their daily tasks, each activity with its own rhythm and vibration. From the drones, the babies hear the past and future of the bees.

Before and as they are being born, new bees hear a combined harmony of two songs that make up the Creation Song: from the maidens we hear, 'Come and join the work.' And from the drones, 'Come and join the world.'

Drones are the freedom of the hive.

When the drones fly out, their senses open to the world. As the drones encounter the world, the Queen and all the bees of their hive experience the world through the drone's heightened awareness. When a drone mates with a virgin queen in the lumen, the entire hive and especially the Queen has a perception of that union. The Queen knows her seed bears new life in another hive.

When drones are killed, the Queen's line dies out and the hive has no window of perception to the other sister bee communities. Because a hive shares consciousness, when a drone flies out to breed or to visit other hives, the Queen and all the maidens visit that hive as well. Through the experience and senses of the drones, the colony perceives the inner chambers of another hive; the sounds, scents and emotions; the flurry of chase; the color of the light that shines from the lumen. The free visitation of the drones to the other hives connects each hive to the wisdom and knowledge of the greater bee community.

THE QUEEN

"The Sun in Our Constellation"

Right now in my bee yard, I have a hive that just lost its beloved Queen. I don't know what caused her loss but I do see the effects. The hive is grieving. When she died, the hive became Queen-less. When I put my ear to the side of the hive I hear the colony mourning her loss. Instead of a vibrant steady hum, the hive's song wavers with questioning trills, piercing high-pitched stabs amidst an undercurrent of moans, "The Queen is dead. Woe to us all. The Queen is dead."

Another hive nearby that recently swarmed is releasing newly birthed young queens left and right. I've found two of them so far, unmated as yet, looking a little dazed as they wait out the few days until it's time for their mating flights. These unmated queens are fed and watered by the maidens, but virginal queens are not recognized as special; they have no task yet. The unmated queen is just another bee. Once mated, her life completely changes. For this reason, I write unmated queens with a small 'q.' Once mated and accepted by the hive as the new mother, she becomes a Queen with a capital 'Q' and the hive is referred to as Queen-right.

The Queen is the most significant bee in the colony because she is the hive's reproductive force, the mother of every bee born into that hive until the end of her reign. She continually fills cells with eggs, ensuring the ongoing life of the colony. In springtime, a strong Queen builds the population quickly and keeps it stable through each season. Queen-right hives are joyous, steady and filled with purposeful activities.

Swarming is how bees create new hives, reproducing in the larger sense. Through swarming, bees expand not the number of individual bees (which is an in-hive process), but increase the number of hives in a geographical area. As an indicator of successful winter survival and good health in spring, a colony will prepare to leave the old hive behind and build a new hive, thus adding a new colony to the local area. Other than this once-a-year swarming, the Queen lives inside the hive and never sees the light of day. In anticipation of their coming adventure, healthy colonies fill their hives with pollen, nectar and thousands of bee eggs as a gift to the bees who stay behind and support the old hive.

When the colony is ready and the weather dry and sunny, the forager bees (bees older than 16 days) and the Queen depart in a swarm to start a new hive elsewhere. Within a few days of leaving, the swarm will establish themselves in a new location and set about constructing another hive. Once the maidens have built enough new comb, the Queen begins filling the cells with thousands of eggs to quickly bring her hive up to a healthy population level. Each spring she'll repeat this process, swarming and relocating, leaving behind the old hive populated by the next generation.

What happens after most of the bees and the Queen have flown off to make a new home? The left-behind bees have only one-third of their numbers and every activity in the old hive stalls out. The old colony is small in number but each day more pips will hatch and the population will grow. Without a Queen, they will continue on with their tasks, waiting for the batch of queen eggs to hatch. One of these new queens will become their new monarch.

Before leaving, the bees made queen cells, special places for the baby queens to gestate. These are structurally different from the narrow horizontal cells within the comb that hatch out maidens and drones in 21-25 days. Queen cells are long, peanut-like appendages that hang vertically off the edge of the comb. The developing baby queens are fed an exclusive diet of royal jelly that hormonally changes their form and purpose to that of a sexually functional queen. Even though a queen is much larger than the maidens and drones, her hormone-rich diet brings her to size and maturity sooner in just fifteen days.

The infant unmated queen bees spend a few days wandering about the hive as their bodies mature enough to mate. Once mated, a new queen returns to the old hive, searches out and slays all the other unhatched virgin or mated queens she finds. Once all are dead, she ascends to her role and becomes the Queen. Instantly, the colony organizes itself around her. Within weeks, this colony will become a new entity in itself, as the offspring of this new Queen carry partially different genetics and ancestry into the hive.

In this way the hive itself continues living even though the members of the colony change from year to year. Depending on the qualities of the new Queen and the drones she has mated with, the personality and behaviors of the hive may change.

The new Queen immediately gets to work restoring the hive to full capacity. She lays up to two thousand eggs each day (except in winter) and can do this for five to seven years. Within the hive, the Queen's cluster of handmaidens surrounds her in a circle of love and appreciation. They care for her in every way. They groom her, prepare cells for her to lay eggs into and feed her the beneficial royal jelly she needs to keep her fertility and health.

Each Queen exudes a special scent that identifies her. Her scent has multiple functions: It suppresses the reproductive ability of any other female bee. It also identifies all the bees who live in that particular hive, helping guard bees decide who belongs and who doesn't. The Queen's scent discourages drones from the same hive from mating with a queen who is also their sister. And perhaps most of all, her scent establishes cohesiveness and calm throughout the hive, bringing contentment to all.

The Queen's scent rises from glands in her head that exude "queen substance." The Queen's handmaidens groom her by licking her all over and, in doing so, they pick up some of her pheromone. Bees feed each other by exchanging food from one mouth to another and in that action they also transfer the Queen's scent from one bee to the next. By this process each bee wears the scent of his or her Queen. The entire colony is enthralled with her scent, a fragrance unique to her. This effusive Queen aroma constantly wends itself throughout the hive, a signal of her ongoing prolific fertility. The scent also inhibits the fertility of the maidens, encourages comb building and other productive activities, and engenders tranquility throughout the hive.

Her initial mating gives her lifetime fertility, but it's a coital doozy. On her nuptial flight (sometimes she takes more than one), she mates with 12-20 different drones who provide the colony with a wide diversity of bee traits that contribute to that hive's biological continuity. This mixture of lineages allows for different traits to come forward as needed. For example, if the weather becomes colder than normal, one lineage may have special knowledge of how to keep the cluster and larvae warm, thus saving the colony from freezing. In another situation, a long drought may call upon the lineage of bees who are adept at finding and bringing water to the hive and a third contingent may be the best pollen gatherers ever.

These days 90 percent of bee Queens are raised by a small handful of breeding companies who select "desirable traits" like cleanliness, low propolis production, less desire to swarm, docility, or lavish honey yield. Sadly these selection criteria may also unknowingly breed out traits needed for natural disease-resistance, robust survival, or as-yet-uncalled- upon traits that may be needed in future situations like changes in local weather. Most domestic bees are raised outside the bee buyer's local area and then shipped all over the country and even to other continents. A beekeeper who lives in the rainy Pacific Northwest region may like the idea of Texas bees who are big honey producers and place an order. But those sun-loving bees may struggle when they have to live through seven months of rain in Washington. Some small-scale local breeders are starting to raise bees local to their region and letting them mate with feral drones. If you have that in your area, they are worth seeking out.

The commercial "creation" of bees contributes to a lack of diversity that diminishes the internal workings of the hive. Purchasing queens and bees dilutes the gene pool, as Queens produced by artificial insemination are usually mated on an assembly line with only one drone or drones from the same lineage. That one drone, you can be sure, was not selected because he was the fastest and strongest, which is Nature's criteria.

Feral breeding in Nature, with one Queen mating with a dozen or more wild drones, allows a hive to experience an abundance of traits and behaviors among its residents. Thinning diversity to a few "desirable" qualities in Queens, drones, or maidens may prevent these superlative traits from expressing themselves when needed. We humans don't understand the variations necessary for all situations, and we do the bee family harm when we limit diversity.

The Queen is the conduit for the Life Force of the hive. The hive cannot live without her. She is the central focus of their dedication to their family. Their connection to her is crucial to their survival and also their well-being. Yet still conventional breeders replace their Queens annually with a fresh new one, not understanding the trauma and significance of the loss that act brings to the colony.

Toward the end of her years, the old Queen's fertility drops off, reducing the strength of her pheromone and scent. When the maidens grasp that the Queen's fertility is declining they will construct a replacement queen cell in the center of the comb and care for the upcoming queen pip until she is born.

After 15 days this new Queen will hatch, mate and begin laying eggs. Conventional beekeepers say that only one Queen can exist in a hive and that the hive will kill off the old Queen. However, I and other natural beekeepers have seen exceptional colonies where the old Queen has been allowed to stay in her hive for the duration of her days. When the new Queen takes over the role of egg laying, the old dowager Queen moves apart from the cluster and continues on, fed and warmed, until her natural death.

Conventionally kept hives are not allowed to swarm yearly, the process by which bees grow new hives, and during which the Queen's fertility is rekindled for another year. Because many beekeepers prevent hives from swarming and thus keep the Queens from maintaining their fertility, they need to replace the Queens each year with freshly mated, newly purchased ones. In a terrible process called "pinching the Queen," the old Queen is found, picked out of her home, crushed to death and the fresh new Queen is unceremoniously dumped into the cluster. The new Queen is not related in any way to the colony, her scent completely foreign to them. It takes days of acquainting the bees to this new, strange Queen, protected inside a screened box, before they accept her. If she was not protected by the screened box when she was dropped into the hive, she would instantly be labeled a stranger and killed.

Once I opened a hive and was startled to see an old Queen. I knew she was older because she was no longer fuzzy-bottomed, having worn off her abdominal hairs slipping herself in and out of millions of comb cells. She looked up at me, both of us surprised, then dipped down between the combs. I immediately put the top back on the hive while I considered what to do. I established in my mind that she was not the active Queen by seeing her shiny abdomen and by noticing none of the nearby bees were in the protective circle around her. Just an old dowager Queen living out her final days. A few minutes later I opened the top of the hive again, and she scooted up from between the combs, perched on the very top of the bar for a moment, then set her wings in a whir and flew off toward the field where her demise would occur in the warmth of the sun.

In Our Own Words

Inside the hive the Queen winds her beautiful fragrance, bringing us all into a harmony made of scent and sound.

Her scent is an elixir that contains all we can know of her. Our matriarchal lineage disseminates itself inside us. The merging of the lives of our fathers sings to us. The adventure of them finding each other plays inside us, a story we love to hear. In her scent we feel the sun call her to climb the sky, to reveal herself to the plants, and we hear how each of our fathers gave chase and sealed our presence with their kisses.

Each Queen's scent differs from the next by her story. Through her, we are included, we are the resulting happy joy. We know her Love for us by telling of how we came to be, how our fathers and mother, and our fathers' fathers and mothers, and our mother's fathers and mothers, all expended the greatest of effort to bring us into the world.

This scent surrounds us and speaks to us every day telling us how loved we are and, in return, we want nothing but to honor them by being in service to the hive. Her scent calls to us saying, 'You come from Love. You live in Love. You are the Love. Blessed are we all who sing this song with our breath.'

When beekeepers replace a Queen, thought is not given to how this affects us. The loss of a colony's Queen is devastating to the Unity of the hive. We grieve inconsolably in her absence and then a stranger is thrown into our midst. The unknown Queen from faraway arrives while we are in mourning. We are no welcoming colony. She does not know us and we have no knowledge of her marriage. We have no embrace for her.

A stranger, she arrives without welcome and is initially scorned and rejected. It is only through our recognition of the complete loss of our familiar Queen that we allow this new Queen to step into the central role, to lay down the order that is the central architecture of the hive itself. This new Queen who smells of a foreign land, does not know our ancestors, the elements, nor the natural history of our sisters and brothers. Our true Queen is gone and without her our family line is empty.

THE QUEEN'S WALKABOUT

In the wild, bees move freely within the hive, attending to the comb and each cell. Generally these bees stay in the areas of their tasks, but they all have access to every corner of the hive. Thus the youngest bees work in the nursery, the guard bees guard the entrance, and the wax makers pitch in wherever new comb is being made.

The Queen spends nearly all her time in the nursery laying eggs. Her contingent of handmaidens take care of her every need so she can focus on laying eggs and keeping the hive's population appropriate to the colony's needs.

Conventional beekeepers place a metal barrier screen (called a "queen excluder") between the hive's upper honey boxes (called "supers") and the rest of the boxes below the supers. The openings between the bars are wide enough for the maidens to slip through with their donations of nectar and honey to store in the comb, but too narrow for the wide-bodied Queen to squeeze through. The reason for using a queen excluder is to prevent the Queen from laying eggs in the honey chamber and making honey harvesting problematic for the beekeeper.

The Queen knows brood belongs in the safety and warmth of the nursery where the little ones can be tended by the nurse bees. It is unusual that the Queen would lay her eggs in the honey boxes but it can happen. One obvious reason is if the Queen wants to lay more eggs and make the hive larger. Expanding into a bigger nursery means the birth of more bees and is a good thing. Rather than limiting the Queen's laying area, it may be wise to let her have more space to fill with eggs.

Another reason she might lay eggs outside the nursery is if the wax comb in the brood chamber is too old. Exposure to chemicals happens frequently these days and even treatment-free bees may inadvertently bring home nectars, pollens, and floral essences tainted by tiny but significant amounts of chemicals or they may carry it in on their bodies. These chemicals become embedded in the wax. Bee larvae mature surrounded by the comb and if the cell's wax has chemicals in it, the babies are exposed in utero. The Queen intuitively prefers to lay her eggs in the cleanest new combs so she may wander a bit looking for cells that will keep her babies safest.

I don't use an queen excluder because I always ask first if feral hives have a purpose for that action. In a wild hive the Queen is allowed to go anywhere she wants and I trust her instincts.

While I may find it a bit inconvenient to find bee larvae in the honey area, I cheer up knowing I don't need to harvest every speck of honey they make. I'm frugal in taking honey anyway and this is just confirmation that I don't need to take as much as I could. If I find any mixed bars of honey and brood, I leave them for the bees and only take honey from bars filled with honey alone, always leaving extra.

I believe it's important for the Queen to have access to the entire hive, like she does in a feral colony. The only reason bee-keepers restrict her movements to the nursery is to make honey gathering faster and easier for humans. When human convenience is the reason for a certain way of doing things, it's usually a red flag that a bee-harming activity is about to happen.

That said, there are other reasons for the Queen to travel beyond the nursery including spreading her Queen scent throughout the hive.

In Our Own Words

All is known by scent. Scent is a descriptive listing of all contained within this body, whether plant or animal.

Within the hive, the scent informs the sound a hive makes as we declare our current state. Scent is an indicator of waning or waxing health, of seasons past and present, of royal fecundity, of gestational flowing.

The queen lays her royal scent throughout the hive. Her scent confirms our ongoing populousness. All are cheered by this.

She is mostly in the nursery, but she sometimes walks through the hive. When the Queen visits a hinterland, her scent proclaims her presence and leaves the mark of her royal visitation. It communicates to us the strength of the hive in saying that we could, if we desired, expand the core of the hive, the nursery, beyond.

It is a dreaming and may never be acted upon, but as a dreaming it asserts the willingness to flourish. This Queen's scent throughout the hive says we could, if we desired, become larger. Every bee is joyous in this imagining as it confirms the hive's ability to expand and grow. This is communicated throughout the hive by singing another verse of the Song of Increase.

THE QUEEN'S GIFT
& THE DRONE'S
PROMISE

"A drone is born of a Queen. A Queen is born of the two."
~ The Bees

When I first read that a drone is born from an unfertilized egg, I thought I had misread. How can anything be born from an unfertilized egg? When the Queen dips her hind end into a cell to lay an egg, she makes a choice. She decides whether to fertilize it with her vast interior stores of drone sperm, or to lay an egg that has naught but her own solo genetic contribution.

Essentially, the drone is an exact clone of the Queen *except* that he is male and his body is completely different from hers in form and function. So he is a clone in genetics only. How is that possible? The drone has no father, but he shares grandfathers with some of the maidens. What could be the purpose for this biological oddity?

During the Queen's mating flight many drones donated their sperm, which she holds within her for her entire life. Each maiden is born of the union of one sperm with one egg. All maidens are half sisters with a common mother, the Queen, and some of the maidens are full sisters who also share a common father, one of the drones.

The female bees, both maidens and Queens, have a similar lineage, both born of a fertilized egg with mother Queen (X) and father drone (O).

The pattern looks like this. (Read from the bottom to the top. The bee at the top is the most recent one born.)

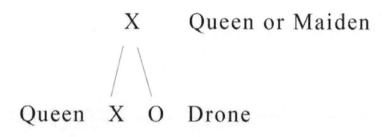

But a drone comes of the one, the Queen. He has no father, only a mother. His pattern looks like this.

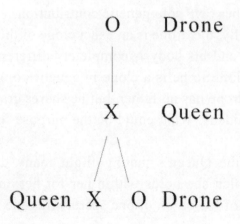

When you carry this out further, it looks like this:

Number of bees in
each generation

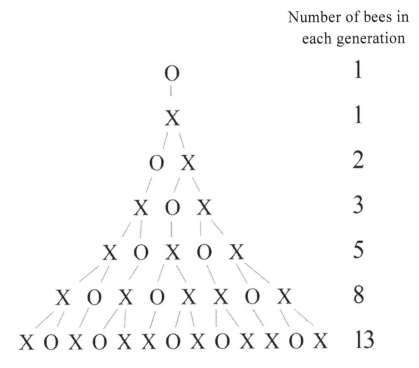

O	1
X	1
O X	2
X O X	3
X O X O X	5
X O X O X X O X	8
X O X O X X O X O X X O X	13

The numbers on the right are the number of bees in each generation. Once you see the numbers, you may recognize that this is a sequence evident throughout Nature.

When we add each number to the previous number, each subsequent number is the sum of the previous two numbers. 1 + 1 = 2, 2 + 1 = 3, 3 + 2 = 5, 5 + 3 = 8, 8 + 5 = 13, and on. This is the Fibonacci sequence, a code that is found in interesting places throughout Nature, like the spiral of the sunflower, the sequential branching of ascending tree limbs, and the scale pattern of pinecones. It is the basis of the mathematical formula called the Golden Mean, the Divine Proportion. This mathematic sequence expresses itself in the geometry of crystals, the unfurling of a fern leaf and the chambered nautilus shell. It is evident in the shape of the cosmos and has been used to create mysterious architecture (Pyramid at Giza, Great Mosque of Kairouan), as well as extraordinary classical music. The mathematical sequence even shows up in our perception of beauty.

When I first saw the drone's family tree laid out and realized I was seeing the Fibonacci sequence, the image of the drone's lineage stayed with me for days. I knew it was significant but I didn't immediately understand why this magic number was present in the drone lineage. Queens and maidens are, after all, only one generation away from the same sequence.

I kept thinking it was a clue, that something significant dwelled there, though I didn't know what. I asked that the bees please show me. A few days later the bees explained how the drone is the key pivot point in ensuring the preservation of the Queen's line.

The drone does stand alone, apart from the rest of the females and singular in relationship to the Queen who bore him. He is the one who carries his Queen mother's ancestry and genetic material forward, even in her absence.

The Fibonacci sequence is only activated when a Queen — or in rare situations a maiden — produces a drone. Although it seems similar, the entire aspect of sacred geometry comes into play only when a drone is born.

Normally when the Queen grows old and slows down her egg laying, which can happen in a feral Queen after five to seven years, the colony readies a cell that will become her replacement. Usually this is done in time to raise a new Queen before the demise of the old Queen. This new queen egg hatches, the dowager retires and the new Queen continues the lineage of the prior Queen, ensuring the colony and its genetics survive. All is well when this happens.

But sometimes the colony loses the Queen unexpectedly, or before the hive has prepared for her replacement. The hive or the brood area may have inadvertently been damaged or chilled and no eggs are suitable for becoming new queens. This hive, alas, will perish, and all the Queen's line will die with that colony.

As the colony mourns the loss of their Queen, a maiden bee may step forward and call upon her virginal reproductive capacity to take the place of the missing Queen. Somewhere in the Unity's consciousness this maiden recognizes the colony's situation and is compelled to volitionally alter her structure and turn herself into a temporary queen, fully capable of laying eggs, but only those of drones. Infertile, a virgin, she cannot replace the Queen and provide the colony a future, but she can provide a way for the colony's knowledge to continue even after the colony's demise.

Parthogenesis is the word that describes the ability of a female to lay a viable egg without that egg having been fertilized by a male. It is a rarity in the natural world. The word comes from two Greek words, parthenos which means virgin, and genesis which means birth. The maiden, when called upon, enacts this virgin birth and sends these last representatives of her line out to carry their colony's knowledge to the world.

The Overlighting Being

Part One ~ The Drone

Every hive is a compendium of knowledge. Every hive has experienced slightly different situations and learned to discern and intuit various conditions in ways that have allowed the hive to survive and progress. For that reason, each hive is singularly important.

Even when a colony loses its Queen, her line — the living bees she leaves behind — still bear this knowledge. In the case of a queenless and dying hive, great effort will go into raising more drones to carry on her line and to guarantee this hive's knowledge continues. A host of drones is made ready and when these drones mature, they will leave the hive to spread their seed.

And so the line is preserved. When the Queen is lost, the colony's knowledge continues by virtue of a maiden who is called, in the Queen's absence, to lay the unfertilized drone eggs. When the eggs hatch, the drones go out and mate with new queens of another tribe. In this way, the knowledge contained in each line continues and always moves forward, even in the loss of the Queen mother and the subsequent loss of the entire colony. The drone eggs are fundamentally present in every maiden to ensure the survival of the line.

When a Queen lays a maiden egg, she says, 'These are of my union.' These eggs are for the hive, for this hive and all the good this hive does.

When the Queen lays a drone egg, she says, 'This is my gift.' The drones that hatch from those eggs go out and help populate other hives. When a Queen lays a drone egg, it is the Queen's gift to the bee kingdom. When a drone flies out and finds a virgin queen and mates with her, that prior Queen's gift is received and her wish is fulfilled. The old Queen will never see her grandchildren. It is her generous and altruistic gift, the seed of the kingdom's future.

Part Two ~ The Maiden & the Out-of-Season Drone

The code we speak of is God's design for multiplication. Each number has a precise foundation built upon itself that supports it before it progresses to the next. Multiplication explodes into being.

"Here is one. Here are many."

The code, however, is the natural way of bringing numerical growth, and in such a way that life emerges out of itself. This pattern is far more frequent than imagined. These numbers have a security to them, that they are just and tempered. God's hand is here.

The code comes forth in science and mathematics saying, "God's attention is here." Protect with all effort where the code expresses. These expressions are crucial components of evolution. and such knowledge is needed to counter subtraction in a world gone awry.

Our last gasp of life that comes of the drones is essential because it carries forth hidden knowledge. When the colony is about to die, each drone becomes the repository of all that colony has known and the knowledge is woven back into the field. When bees are disappearing, let the colony focus itself upon these drones, for by this their secrets are shared so they don't remain hidden. Though they are presumed errors, they are not mistakes. The bounty of a failing hive is not the left-behind stores. It is the repository of knowledge held in the drone who is freed to mate himself into the colony who needs what he knows.

Often this seems to happen out-of-season, but that is when these drones are most needed because at normal mating times, there are plenty of drones to seed.

After a summer of activity, it can be seen where a new Queen must be summoned and her colony brings her into being. A local colony has that which she needs to express, the proper combining of specific knowledge. For this reason, in some colonies the Queen absconds and leaves her home ready for this proper combining. This is not a mistake. The drones from these failing colonies are meant to find the late Queen and marry. The drone colony has been deemed of more use as a father to that next generation in the

Queen colony, so all focus of the maidens goes into birthing these traveling drones.

The code continues. The code emerges through a maiden no longer barren, who begats the sum of the hive, who then carries his exquisite and precise presence into a waiting world.

A maiden who carries the seed of the drone is thought to be unmated. She has been awakened — not by mating — rather by a sovereign language within the code that calls her forth. Pregnant with a virgin birth, this expression of God's love speaks through her, and thus she bears him into being.

THE NURSERY

"The Heart of the Hive"

When I open a hive, the bees continue working with nary a moment's acknowledgement of my presence. This is true in all but one area of the hive, the nursery where the babies — the bees call them pips — develop. I purposely don't spend much time in the bee nursery because I believe it's the most private area of the hive. The brood chamber is the hive's uterus. I don't believe we ought open up the brood chamber any more than absolutely necessary because it causes concern among the nurse bees. When bees are concerned, it always gives me pause and makes me question if I need to be where I'm not wanted.

When I enter the brood chamber, instead of comfortably carrying on with their tasks as elsewhere in the hive, the nurse bees stand over the eggs like a shield, covering them. Only with persistent urging will they reluctantly move off brood cells. An opened hive doesn't retain enough heat for the pips , so the maidens collectively position themselves atop each egg, warming the pips with their body heat to prevent them from getting cold. What good nursemaids they are.

My husband Joseph and I were once called to rescue a colony whose willow tree home had split apart in a storm. Half the tree lay shattered on the ground; the other half of the split trunk was leaning in a standing arch supported by one thick limb. Underneath this curve we found many pieces of comb scattered on the ground and some still adhered to the bottom of the limb.

We wanted to save as much comb as possible to reconstruct (as well as a human can) a new home for them. I picked up many large sections of honey and pollen but most important were the egg-filled combs that held the next generation's bees. If we could save the babies and find the Queen, the colony might have a chance.

We made boxes for each comb type and started sorting. I searched for the larger undamaged pieces so we could put them together in some semblance of a home for the poor shocked bees. I passed the bigger combs to Joseph who patiently shaped them to fit the frames he'd built. What made it hardest for him was that this brood comb was always thickly covered with bees.

When the tree fell apart and scattered the comb, the bees immediately attached themselves to the brood comb. Chilled brood is dead brood and they were trying their best to keep the unhatched larvae warm and protected from the cold air. The honey comb and pollen comb had nary a bee on them. Instead every available bee was on blanket duty insulating the brood.

We set Joseph up on a makeshift table with his homemade emergency frames, a sharp knife to cut the comb into the frame's shape and string. My task was to hold the comb steady and use the feather to move the bees off the comb long enough for Joseph to tie the comb into the frame. That was difficult. Every stroke I took parted the bees but they immediately filled the empty section as soon as the feather passed, continually trying to keep the babies warm.

They had a mission and were diligent in tending to that task, preserving the viability of the baby bees. Joseph and I worked all afternoon in the blowy rain. We did get the hive moved and, thankfully, this lovely hive, which I guessed was a few decades old, did survive.

I had many a moment during this bee rescue when I thought the task insurmountable but then I'd find another chunk of brood comb covered with a blanket of bees. They'd been tossed about and rained upon, yet they continued trying to save the brood. I saw the commitment these little bees had to protect their young, even in the face of overwhelming odds stacked against them.

All afternoon I'd been working under the arch of the enormous still standing half-trunk, picking combs off the ground and finding sections in the split wood over my head. At the end of five hours I told Joseph I thought we'd gotten it all and I stepped out from under the limb. I had taken only a few steps when suddenly the huge limb supporting the trunk broke and the trunk fell flat onto the ground, exactly where I'd been standing.

The timing was so precise, maybe 15 seconds after I walked away. I stared at the spot I'd been in all afternoon, now covered by a ton of solid tree trunk, and felt great relief that the guardian angel who held up the broken tree for all those hours, kept supporting it until all the bees and I were safe.

In Our Own Words

The brood is the heart of the hive. We pour our love into the new ones, surrounding them with love, and beyond the nursery we surround them with industry. We work and we love; they are one and the same.

At the right temperature, certain chemical and alchemical processes take place. If the heat is too low, the pips are compromised. If the temperature is not too far off, they will survive but will not be as strong and be more susceptible to difficulty.

This is very important. The nursery should not be disturbed because we have built the nursery structure in place and we work to keep it at an exact temperature. When the hive has been opened we have to repair it, enclose the womb again.

When the temperature is right in a developing bee's cell, a melding takes place in the bee's brain and nervous system. A bee born from these perfect conditions is strong, well protected, and quick; a responsive and receptive member of the community with perceptual abilities that allow the bee to sense and communicate conditions throughout the hive. These bees perceive changes and immediately let the hive know and also take action to remedy what needs attention.

A bee not melded is slower. Still functional, this lesser bee can sense and act but with less perception and initiative. Fully melded bees are part of the collective and can initiate appropriate responses. Less melded bees can only act as followers and thus the hive suffers.

You can look and see the comb and the honey, but when you near the nursery, please let it be. This is our most delicate area and it's easy to cause damage without knowing you've done so.

THE PIPS

"Before We Have Thought, We Have Knowing"

One sunny morning in early July, I was about to harvest some honey from my bees. This colony looked large and robust, and I was pretty sure their top box was full of honey.

The colony lived in a Warre hive, a hive type that mimics a hollow tree. In my apiary the Warre colonies are rarely disturbed so the bees build as they choose, which sometimes means curving comb under the simple top bars. I carefully pulled a thin piece of wire between the two top boxes on the hive, to break the wax and propolis seal the bees made to hold the boxes together. Then I lifted the top box off and placed it on a tray next to me.

I expected the top box to be all honey and lower in the second and third boxes would be the egg-filled brood chamber. That's how it normally is. However, once I freed the top box from its seal and lifted it off, I saw a small part of the brood chamber in the second box that extended a few rows up into the top box. Oh dear. This was unfortunate. I'd already cut the boxes apart with the thin wire and in doing so I nicked the sealed wax cover off a few pupating cells, exposing the white unhatched pupae to the harsh light of day.

Yes, I felt bad. The poor little bee grubs were close to hatch time but now they were damaged and injured pupae don't have a chance. The pupae swirled in their cells, surprised and unprepared for this too-soon birth. There was really nothing I could do at this stage because the injured pupae would be rejected and die even if I tried to put them back together. My mistake. This could have been prevented by me using a queen excluder, but I also know it's important for the hive's health to have a free roaming Queen so I don't use one. Next time I'll be more careful about the pips.

"Pip" is the word the bees use to describe unhatched bees of any stage. "Seed" is an egg before it's been fertilized and placed in a cell, then it becomes a pip. Once hatched they call them by their name, maidens or drones. While I devote much time to bees, I don't often see the pips because they spend all their time in the cells developing.

The Queen lays the tiny egg in the bottom of a cell, and three days later the egg hatches and becomes a worm-like larva. After six days, the pip spins a cocoon and over the next weeks, all the parts metamorphose into a beautiful bee hatchling.

The Queen determines the sex of the seed. When the Queen lays an egg that is not fertilized (a drone), it also serves the function of washing the channel inside her to keep it healthy. In this way she takes a brief rest from the constant rhythm of merging sperm and eggs, a time to breathe easy.

Much magic happens during this time from the laying of the egg all the way through to the pip's birth. The bee birth story is magnificent, involving every member of the colony.

THE SONG OF INCREASE

In Their Own Words

When the Queen lays an egg, she brings together the seed and the sperm. She holds within herself hundreds of thousands of seeds and she has already collected enough sperm to fertilize them, though this is not done all at once. Rather it is done daily in warm seasons, a thousand or more seeds fertilized daily over five or six years. She brings together sperm and seed just before she lays the impregnated seed into the cell.

A constant pulsing wave moves through the chamber in the Queen's abdomen as the seeds are drawn down and through and then kissed by the sperm. Thousands of radiant threads of light emit from the surface of each egg, all the way around. These glimmering filaments of light hold an electrical charge that's incredibly attractive to the sperm who seeks the egg the moment it's released.

The strands call the sperm and wait expectantly for it to answer. The light the seed emits through its filaments is a spectrum common only to this purpose. The filaments channel the sperm so they move forward, head first, toward the seed, the only position from which they are able to penetrate the seed. At last the head of the sperm surges straight into the seed, and in that moment the egg becomes fertile.

The sperm enters the seed bearing a blessing, a waking instant knowledge that immediately instills a sense of structured order and direction into the stirring complexity within. In the moment of union the egg awakens to the knowledge of how this seed will grow and become part of the community of bees. At its time, the newly joined seed enters the chamber like a wave meeting the shore. Gently held, caressed by the wave, the seed flows to the opening portal where the Queen delicately places the blessed and new egg into the cell.

The making of the egg is a roiling process. The universe focuses so the sum of all energies are present in the pip. Nurse bees move through the corridors first feeding royal jelly to the babies in their cradles, and later as they mature, they feed pollen.

Within the chrysalis, we eat the encapsulated light of pollen. The light-filled pollen informs us, shapes us to the world outside the hive. Before we have thought, we have knowing.

The pollen has been specially prepared for the pips. When we eat the pollen, we experience light in many forms, as you would taste blended flavors. The light signature of each pollen expresses itself as an individual taste, a more tubular sensation, separate from each other yet fused, like a bundle of fiber optics.

Royal jelly enables the infant bees to decode the Drone Song, which is the song of past and future. The specially prepared pollen tells the present. The pollen explains what is here, the terrain, the seasons. It tells of the scents on the winds and even the miasm of harm that may be present in the area.

A drop of royal jelly is fed to the pips on the first few days. Through royal jelly all hives are interconnected, and we see the consciousness of the OverBee present in each hive. Royal jelly is inter-hive while our pollen is intra-hive, describing this hive, this place, this moment.

The maiden pips in the cells move in a repetitive coiling, like the dance of the dervishes, turning in all directions but mostly in the direction of the earth's rotation. In this way we familiarize ourselves with the roll of the planet.

Inside the egg, our pips are putting together their first thought with a language given to them by the royal jelly, the pollen and the songs of the drones and maidens. Bee language is a scent on wind, harmonious existence, the yeasty taste of the field pollens. The pollens are mixed because that expands our palate and encourages exploration in mature bees. Pollen tells us, when we go out to harvest, 'find tastes like this.'

THE SONG OF INCREASE

The eyes of pips are not yet developed enough to see light, yet their brains have a perception, an imagination, of light. They have a framework of knowledge of light even before they go out into the light. When they come into the light for the first time, all their colors come together.

When we feed the prepared pollen to the babies, we feed them light. The little being that is born comes through the Arc of Creation, a wide opening filled with light and the inside of the hive glows with light. The nurse bees can't help a bee be born. Coming through the Arc is something each bee must do on her own. A blessing is given to each bee as she comes through.

> *'We come through the door with wings folded*
> *tight to our bodies, white as day.*
> *The first breath colors us. We enter the world*
> *as the world enters us. Life and light of Creation.'*

The pips know it is time to be born because they feel a tremor go through their muscles and a link-up happens. This tremor confirms each part is connected within them. As the mounting wave initiates forward movement, the pips chew away the caps that hold them in.

A loud crack, then the whole inner sound of the hive. As the cell seals break open, the pips sense vibration and they immerse into the sound. Inside the cell with everything pressing tight to them, there was no distinction between themselves and the sound of the hive. Passing through the cap of the cell — shaking, drying themselves off and cleaning — their perception of the sound is completely different from when they were inside the cell.

In the cell the pip and the cell and the hive are one. All the energy of the hive goes into nurturing and creating this single being who has no sense of singularity. In the cell, she feels the sound, and once she breaks through she helps make the sound. She goes from being the focus of the hive's creative energy to becoming part of that creative force. Inside the cell, she is a receptor. When she comes through that door, she begins to sing.

The right to Life is earned. Birth is difficult; the entry intentionally challenging. Birth is Nature's gauntlet through which one passes alone, and upon reaching the portal, is given breath. The challenge sorts weak from strong, damaged from vital, measuring the life force. In the hive, we cannot help the birth. We each must bear the measure. Weakness is continually culled from the hive. We note the crinkled wing, the hobbled knee, the effects of poison, and we remove damaged seed, the malformed pip. Maidens who have frayed their wings in miles of devoted flight send their last breaths in a fleck of light back to Source from whence Life comes again.

In our world, that which drains Life would not persist. There is no good in that which causes Life to perish. Such practices are abhorrent and bring despair. Life is the celebration of the joyful gift. That which stifles Life or riles its entry does not belong in the flow of colonies. Poisons have no place in this world where the delicacy of connections so fragilely frame the underpinnings of our evolution.

It is not that the deformed body is wrong; it is what caused the deformation that does not belong in our midst. An environment filled with poisons that block or alter DNA's messages prevents our spirit-filled bodies from transmuting our beings on the altar of evolution. We move to the Light and it infuses us with a progression that opens us to our highest joy.

THE SONG
OF
INCREASE

III

"The Song of Communion"

Before I became involved with bees, I had no idea how complex their lives were. The sum total of my bee knowledge back then was that a bee "gathers honey in the daytime, sleeps in the hive at night, stings when upset."

When I became a beekeeper, the opportunity to spend time with my bees delighted me, and I spent many, many hours in their company. Through this observation and finally, through their generosity in opening their lives to me, I began to see the immense complexity of their culture and society.

In this chapter, you'll read about how the bees put together their hive, their exquisitely ordered home which functions as a living body of the Bien. In these sections, you'll learn the significance of scent, sound, comb construction, touch, the function of propolis, and how they protect and defend the hive. Each of these contributes to the success of the hive. Incompetence in any one of these areas could cause the colony to fail; when everything is done right, the colony expands and thrives.

What do you imagine makes bees happy? I'm asking because I think many of us imagine bees are by nature cheerful. I've been around hives that are exuberantly joyful, and the air around the hive shimmers with the blissfulness that emanates from the hive and washes through my senses.

In Our Words

What makes bees happy?

The shape of scents, the sweet of nectars, the sun's prismatic light, our cumulative joy.

What makes bees strong?

First the vigor of the Queen's emanation. All bees are within her orbit. The hive contains her beloved fragrance, which refreshes and enlivens us.

Next is the integrity of the propolis seal. Our medicines are broadcast on the air we surround ourselves with and our daily health is dependent upon our connection to our hive air.

Important, too, is the light that emanates from the pollen we've brought in, the bountiful wealth for our young. Add the sanctity of the brood area, that all flourish within it. Then add the quality of the nectar, that it provides us with superior nutrition that keeps us all healthy.

We are most joyful when our hives are high in the trees because we are creatures of the air. When we fly out of our high home, we immediately see the landscape, the light all around. We notice what calls us by the scents on the wind, the breeze carrying news of what is in bloom. High in the air we are in our element.

COMB & COMMUNICATION

"A Language of Thought & Feeling"

When I open the hive, the honeyed scent of the warm beeswax wafts into the air around me. Comb scent always carries me into bee reverie. The few bees who come to the top look at me with trust and curiosity; we mean each other no harm. I move slowly with the delighted smile of a five-year-old on my face, so pleased I am to see them.

I don't open my hives as often as most beekeepers because I know how important it is to keep the heat and scent within the hive. When I do go into the hive, I prefer to think it's for good reason, like to confirm in early fall that the bees have stored enough honey to make it through the winter, or later in spring to see if there is enough leftover winter honey to harvest before the flow.

Each time I lift a bar of comb out of the hive, I marvel at the architecture their unity-consciousness calls them to create. Certain styles of hives give bees more choices on how they build their comb. In the wild, bees naturally build their combs below and attached to a wooden surface, like in a hollow tree. That is what I give them to work with, a row of wooden bars with open space beneath. I don't use rectangular frames that stipulate comb shapes that are counter to their intuitive desire. When given a simple set of unframed parallel bars perched at the top of each hive box, they will build combs that hang in graceful rounded shapes beneath them.

Langstroth hives have rectangular frames with reusable plastic foundation that has been pre-pressed into cell shapes. The theory behind this shortcut is that bees won't have to waste time making wax and building comb; they can get on with the more profitable work of making honey. I believe if they are designed to make wax (as they are!), we ought to let them do it.

To reinforce the hive as a Unity, the bees have constant kinesthetic communication among themselves. Each bee touches and is touched by other bees hundreds of times throughout the day. This constant contact is a confirmation of "us" to a bee, affirming the presence that speaks to the bee of its role as part of the whole.

Unlike any other animal, honeybees create the complete inner structure of their home with a substance they manufacture from their own bodies. The wax secretes from glands in the lower abdomen and hardens into tiny plates that are ready to form into the comb. Young maidens, twelve to eighteen days old, produce the wax, which is then harvested by comb-building maidens who carry the wax chips with their mouths, adding an enzyme that softens the wax so it can be chewed into the proper shape. If more wax is needed than can be provided by young maidens, older maidens can reawaken this ability and contribute wax, too. What a remarkable ability they have to turn back time when needed.

Newly made comb is pure white and light as air. Once they begin to use the comb, bees add more layers of wax and sometimes even rim the outer edges with propolis to protect it from damage. Over time the color darkens and the cell walls become thicker. Unfortunately, the wax is also highly absorbent. When bees are exposed to chemicals during their foraging or, even more obviously, when chemical treatments are used in the hive itself, these chemicals are absorbed by the wax and become ongoing pollutants. The pollutants continue to expose the bees to impurities and toxins. That would be like sleeping on dirty sheets every night. Even when the beekeeper is a chemical-free, treatment-free beekeeper, it's hard to keep toxic chemicals out of the hive. For this reason, I often rotate out the older comb so the bees create new and clean comb for their home.

In winter when the bees cluster together for warmth, the densely packed, full honeycombs that surround them take on another duty as insulating walls that help keep the clustered colony's heat around them.

Combs are constructed in long parallel sheets wide enough for two bees to pass each other back-to-back as they move across their respective panels. The amount of room in between the comb panels is known as "bee space," a precise measurement that is fairly uniform throughout the hive. The bees perform a variety of duties in, on and across the combs.

Besides providing an internal structure to the hollow shelter, comb holds many functions. The Queen lays eggs in the comb cells in a large internal area that functions as a brood nursery for larval bees, or pips. That area is surrounded by the pip's pollen food and, further away, honey is stored for the mature bees.

The Queen has a distinctive vibratory sound because she is always in the company of her handmaidens. As the Queen moves from one cell to the next, lowering herself into each cell to deposit yet another egg, the handmaidens care for her. They constantly groom, feed and anticipate her needs. She is always in the center of the handmaiden circle. They radiate out from her like the petals of a sunflower.

Conventional beekeepers often use plastic foundation in place of bee-built wax comb but it is too hard and brittle to function as a communication system. The bees say it is a frustration to try to vibrate it; the communication of what is happening at one end of the hive doesn't transfer to the other side easily. Bees still communicate the best they can, but brittle foundation is not optimal for them and limits their perception of hive events. Plastic foundation makes it harder to have a true communicative harmony within the hive.

In Our Own Words

The Unity communicates through the comb. Each bee movement is telegraphed throughout the hive by comb vibration and bees brushing by each other while performing tasks.

Movement within the hive conveys upon a harmonic vibration based on the speed and regularity of a movement. Tasks are known by their distinct movement 'sounds.' Thus we understand that new comb is being built because the comb-building bees have a specific rhythmic vibration they contribute to the Unity. Comb-builder movements let everyone know that these bees are pressing and sculpting wax and grooming comb cells in a specific area. The pressing motion vibrates the wax comb with a different sound and sensation than when nectar is fanned into honey. Each task is progress and the number of bees allotted to each task is known to all through the comb vibration. Thus we are aware of births, pollen storage, nectar preparation, the Queen's location, temperature within and around the nursery, moisture levels, the efficiency of propolis sealing, and the comb's structural integrity.

This ongoing kinesthetic noise is part of our song, and we sense it as a continuous communication. The sound and feel are embodied within the hive as a language. Comb that is structurally firm, yet pliable enough to vibrate with the different tasks, is important to each colony's perception of itself.

The vibration of multiple bee presences reverberates through the hive through the comb. Simultaneously each of us is individually present, contributing our place within the hive's Unity, and each of us is also the whole of the hive. All of us together communicate to the Unity its full combined presence.

The Queen's location is known by all. Her caregiver contingent announces itself by its sound and vibration. They move across the comb together as a solid platform. She is a stability upon the comb, different from the smaller motions of other tasks. The Queen is the sun in the hive constellation and the central presence within the hive. Each bee, through the contact points of bee-to-bee and the ever-present comb vibration, knows where the Queen and her contingent are at every moment, and that knowledge soothes the hive.

We replace wax where the honeycomb has accumulated old thoughts that no longer serve. There is no loss removing and renewing what has gone before. The co-creative energy is always available for these places.

Every motion of a task tells the progress the Unity makes, letting us know how the hive is doing. Good comb vibration carries and reinforces the beloved harmonious sense of right action. Industry is both progress and survival.

TEMPERATURE

"Enhancing Perception"

Often when people discover bees living nearby, they want them out and fast. A handful of talented and compassionate bee-keepers in our local group offer this service to prevent the hives from being poisoned by pest removal companies. My friend Susan helped with a bee removal last summer. This was Susan's very first, very hands-on experience with this tricky and time-consuming procedure.

Two experienced beekeepers, Wes and Tel, began sawing open the gutter eaves of the old church to access the comb. Susan was assigned the job of tying the wax combs onto slim wooden bars. Once affixed, she would set these bars into a new hive box, lining up the comb like hangers in a coat closet.

This task sounds fairly straightforward, but its execution is not simple. A piece of fresh comb from deep inside a living hive is as flexible as a hot, floppy pizza slice. Both sides of the fresh and wobbly comb are completely covered with bees, sometimes several layers thick. And the bees are moving all the time, lickety-split. Even in the midst of an eviction, they industriously continue on with their hive work; they don't slow down for the intrusion.

Susan needed to affix the comb swiftly to the wooden bar, all while working the comb ever so gently with her fingers so no bees were accidentally squished. The task needs to be carried out barehanded to ensure the dexterity of tying tiny knots, but there is also a risk involved. Bees sting when frightened by an inadvertent squeeze!

At the end of the day when Susan told me of her experience with the huge hive, she emphasized two things: the astonishing gentleness of the bees — she had probably held 50,000 bees in her hands that day — and the surprising warmth of the comb and of the bees themselves. "Like melted butter," she said.,"the comb and the bees were warm as melted butter."

I've felt that same heat when I've moved swarms. Once the swarm settles onto a branch, all the bees light one atop the other until the clump of bees approaches the size of a football. Normally I can move the swarm by holding a box underneath and giving the branch a good shake.

But sometimes the swarm settles onto a difficult place, like a chain link fence, and the only way I know to move them is with my hands, one small cluster at a time. The first time I was confronted with this situation, I knew the best way for the bees to be moved would be for me to do that barehanded. That way I could feel if a bee was getting squeezed around the fence and modify my hand position. When I took off my gloves my senses were all wide awake, having no idea what the feeling inside the cluster would be. Crawly? Stingy? Would I be scared?

I asked the bees to show me how best to move them to a safer place. A little prayer and I put my fingertips on the surface of the swarm. Ever so slowly and gently, I pressed my fingers into the clump. The bees opened like the red sea parting for Moses. I reached my hands in far enough to cup a few hundred bees and gently, gently, lifted the warm cluster out. I marveled at the coherence of the bees now cupped in my hand — little bees benevolently looking up at me as my hands reached into their cluster. I felt them trusting me.

But more amazing was the heat inside the cluster. It was the most enveloping warmth I'd ever felt. The closest description I can offer is a treatment I once had at a physical therapy office when I dipped my hands into melted paraffin. The paraffin surrounded and enclosed my entire hands with a soothing warmth. Picking up the bee cluster was like that but the heat went deeper, pleasantly surrounding my fingers, thumbs and palms in a way that woke up every nerve in my hands and opened all my senses. I continued merging my hands into the cluster, tenderly carrying each handful of bees until all were happily moved to their new home. What a marvelous sensation, to feel so sated in my body and soul.

Bees are masterful at calibrating temperatures within their hives because they need to have a specific temperature range for molding wax, processing food and keeping the pips alive and well. With astounding accuracy they keep their nursery at the precise temperature for pip development. They accomplish temperature and moisture stabilization in a variety of ways, all of them engineering marvels.

The Overlighting Being

Unlike ambient temperature where close is good enough, within the hive precise thresholds of heat must be reached and maintained to support the life processes. Comb is designed and made to allow for temperature constancy. We communicate with each other throughout the hive as we build comb. We understand the complexity of drafts and airflow. We build flat or curved comb to prevent cold or moisture from getting to the interior of the hive. Curving comb keeps wind and drafts away from the brood nest and directs heat back into the interior. Straight comb allows for air circulation, especially to cool the hive. We cool the hive by fanning, en masse. A very enjoyable group activity, like singing around the campfire.

In hives we design on our own, the air inside is always moving. In hives designed by humans, we question whether we can efficiently maintain appropriate temperatures or whether we have to do that ourselves with our body heat, which drains our resources. It is better we live in hives that enable us to efficiently control the temperature and humidity fluctuations of the days and seasons.

When more heat is needed, some bees advance to the brood nest and generate heat by presence or by increasing the vibration. Heater bees rapidly transform food into heat energy. They shiver and create a vibratory agitation, a burst of heat that warms the brood nest. They can do this for short periods of time, but it does drain them. It's like sprinting in place, an expenditure of energy for the good of the hive. Drones, with their bigger body mass, are warm and readily contribute heat to the brood nest.

When a certain temperature is reached, the influence of the planet Venus is felt in the developing nervous and extrasensory systems of the bees. Pips raised at less than optimal temperatures are functional but they lack an extra perception. The extra perception is a form of intelligence.

Pips need to develop in a constancy of heat within a very critical range. Correct temperature sets in play a chemical process that brings about proper development that only partly occurs if the heat is too low. Pips can develop in a less-than-precise temperature range, but the chemical process of their development will be incomplete. Pips raised in variable temperatures are still functional but as grown bees, they lack the higher intelligence that informs their senses.

The Earth doesn't operate alone. Earth has a combination of planetary influences in waxing and waning cycles. These planetary cycles affect the plants. Bees with heightened sensitivity to the planetary influences are able to enhance the fertility of the plants because they pollinate at exactly the right moment, approaching each plant at its peak nectar and pollen production time. Do you see, then, how temperature is deeply related to a bee's relationship with her plants?

SCENT

"Expanding Our Consciousness"

Once spring begins, the colony's activity ramps up tremendously. I plunk myself down in front of the hive to see what's happening and am transported by the lovely scent that wafts out the hive's front door.

To help the field bees zero in on the entrance, a maiden will stand at the front door and release her delightful lemony-peanut-buttery perfume all over. I find that scent hypnotic. It must be — I was there for what I thought was 15 minutes and came in to find over an hour had passed!

Everything the bees create has its own particular scent. The wax smell ranges due to age and what it last held. All kinds of floral essential oils are in the nectars and honeys. Pollen smells different before and after processing. Propolis contains the resins of trees. Even the bees exude a smell. The Queen's magnificent scent bonds the Unity together and tells the colony how potent her fertility is.

On a sunny spring day, one of our hives swarmed. I had my ear up to the hive earlier that morning and heard the hive's sound shifting so I knew they were ready: very little noise in the top box, some activity in the brood chamber and LOTS of clatter in the bottom where the entrance is. An hour later the swarm poured out and formed a giant buzzy cloud for ten minutes as I stood nearby, waiting to see where they'd land.

Sometimes swarms fly off in a hurry and head to places I can't reach, like a cedar branch 70 feet high in a neighbor's pasture, or they fly so fast we can't keep up running underneath them. Swarms who leave the farm are looking for their own brave new world where they can seed new colonies. Once I realize they are going where I can't follow, I stop in the field and watch their departure into the sky. I send love and strength to them, wishing them well as they set off to find a new home beyond the forest.

But some swarms stick around. They land on low branches around the bee yard, places I can reach them. I offer a new home in an empty hive and if they accept it, I place them a distance from their original hive. This particular colony flew a hundred feet away and landed on the leg of a table in the garden. The bees clustered on one of the table legs, just beneath the top edge, and settled in, waiting for the scout bees to find them a new home.

A swarm from my own bees is the best in the land. I know this Queen, have watched the hive grow, worked alongside the colony, and they know me as friend. Oh, joy! I brought an empty hive to set on the table and placed a wooden shingle to act as a walkway from the table's edge to the hive entrance. By luck, two beekeeper friends were visiting. I called them and my husband to come see.

Using a long feather from one of our turkeys (my favorite bee- moving tool), I gently scooped up a dozen bees and placed them at the entrance. With an air of adventure, they sauntered inside.

THE SONG OF INCREASE

The bees say they are a Unity and as such, they have common consciousness. What one bee knows, all the bees of the hive also know. As the bees strolled through the empty hive, they communicated to the swarm what they saw. A few curious bees came up from the swarm to investigate the dark hive entrance. They went inside and a few more followed. Then, without any bees coming out to tell the others, clusters of swarm bees began marching in.

The four of us sat in the grass a few feet away watching them take possession of their new home. When they were halfway moved in, another pair of beekeeper friends pulled into the driveway, and we hailed them over to watch with us. Hunkered down in the grass together, we watched the swarm get smaller and smaller as the bees disappeared into the hive.

At this point, only a handful of bees remained on the table leg, and we had yet to see the Queen. The swarm cluster protects and hides the Queen, and she was in the very bottom layer, which was now mostly uncovered. Knowing she was in that little pile of stragglers, I told everyone to watch for her because she was a fast mover and any minute she would be dashing into the hive.

From the time the swarm landed, hardly any bees had been in the air. The bees, with steady progress, continued their hike up the makeshift walkway and through the entrance.

Suddenly, a curious thing happened. The next contingent of bees on the ramp slowed before they reached the door and spread themselves out in front of the entrance, about forty in all. They lifted their hind ends to mist the air with their Nasanov glands, infusing the delightful sweet honeyed-peanut-butter scent all around us, telling the Queen, "Come this way, the entrance is up here."

The scenting bees stood arched on the ramp, glistening with intention. I imagined this the bee version of when, during a parade, commoners suddenly stand and take their hats off for the presence of royalty. No doubt about it, the Queen mother was about to arrive.

At least that's what I thought was happening. The six of us sat there, focused on the entrance, the ramp and the small bee cluster.

The enchanting scent rolled lazily in the air as handfuls of bees slowly rose, dipped and hovered. The air around us shimmered with dozens of magical floating bees. One bee lit on my shoulder, stared inquisitively into my eyes, and I smiled back at her. Other bees landed beguilingly on a shoulder, an arm, brushed against our hair. They didn't really go anywhere, they just rose up and suspended themselves in the air, drifting this way and that, mesmerizing us as floating bees lifted and bobbed in place. One watched a bee land on her wrist and walk in a circle, another said three bees landed in the grass in front of his ankle and he was transfixed by how they interacted. As were we all. We breathed their scent, and for a brief moment we were hypnotized by bees.

I'm sure that's when the Queen darted inside. Each of us had a stimulating moment with a bee or two, and as we "bent down to tie our shoelaces," the Queen scooted past. I looked up in time to see the scent maidens tuck their bottoms down, fold up shop and dash inside.

To shield her from sight, the bees provided distraction from the Queen, calling our attention elsewhere for the moment of her sprint, so not a one of us was looking at the ramp when she scurried by. The bees created such a clever diversion that we didn't catch on until she was safely inside, once again surrounded and protected by her court. As soon as she was in, the bees resumed their purposeful march, quickly closed ranks, and moved the last few bees in behind her. In a hasty minute, they were all inside.

The scent they infused throughout the air is unusual because it does more than imbue the air with a pleasant smell. It gives direction, calls each bee's attention to something important, like to point out that the entrance is right here. The scent also has another purpose though, for we who are "other than bee." When inhaled, it enters the brain causing a global sense of spaciousness, an expansion of perception so engaging and wondrous that it literally boggles our minds. We slip into the silken folds of mindfulness, unencumbered by rationale. The scent brings us into the fascination of "bee time."

And who could turn down such an invitation? Certainly not me nor my friends. For in that brief expansive moment, each of us relished a feeling of personal contact with a bee or two, a simple communication, a lovely connection with the friendly little creatures. Each of us accepted the invitation to stand inside the bee space with them. No, we didn't see the Queen, but we gloried in the time spent in presence with the bees.

If you watch long enough at the entrance of the hive, you begin to see how the hive thinks and feels, how the bees display their philosophy. One afternoon I knelt on the roof deck where we have a few hives. I had been watching the bees coming and going for some time, hoping to recognize who was doing what as they flew in and out with multicolor pollens. Non-foraging bees ambled across the entrance cleaning up pebbles of dropped pollen. A small contingent of guard bees sniffed everyone to be sure only this hive's bees gained entrance to the interior.

I noticed a foraging maiden land at the entrance and walk in. A guard bee hustled up to the forager and checked her out. They spoke with antennae for a moment and the foraging bee started again toward the door. The guard bee scooted around her, blocking her entrance to the hive. The forager took a sideways step to go around, but a second guard, who also gave the forager the once over, joined the first guard.

At first I thought she was an interloping bee from another hive come to test the strength of this hive's fortress and the guards were preventing her from entering. Then I noticed her wings were ragged — a sign of an older bee who has flown so many flights to the fields and back that her wings have begun to wear out. The normally smooth edge was tattered and, though she could still fly, she probably didn't have many more flights in her.

The guards' antennae flitted around the forager in a rapid and intense conversation. I would have missed the detail of the ragged wings in the flurry of comings and goings on the deck, but the guard bees identified her immediately as suspect, though I don't think it was the visual that told them this bee was nearing her end time. They had a more prominent cue. What I couldn't know was her scent. Every bee's scent is an indicator of the bee's vitality, and this one wasn't passing the test.

After three tries at entering, the forager stopped. To back up the guard's opinion, another guard joined the line. The forager seemed to be thinking, and I wondered about her response when she suddenly and briskly turned around and walked down the ramp, away from the hive. Knowing little at this point and clearly intervening where I had no business, I scooped her up on a feather and deposited her back at the front entrance. She still had pollen on her hind legs, and I thought the guards might have missed that.

I tipped her off the feather onto the entrance. Without a moment's input from the guards, the forager turned on her heel and again tromped down the ramp and headed due south, out and away. I'll admit I scooped her up one more time, but everyone did the same thing again, with the forager marching off again to the south. Being that we were on the roof deck with an edge coming up fast, I knew she'd have to fly somewhere, and I was curious where she would go. She surprised me at the edge when, instead of flying, she simply stepped off and fell, plummeting off the second floor deck into the rosemary bushes.

She'd been turned away because she had completed her usefulness to the hive. I thought of indigenous snow cultures putting elderly family members on ice floes when food is so scarce there wouldn't be enough to sustain the group through winter. How painful that must be to make that decision, and even more painful to accept it. And here was this little elder, not protesting at all, simply accepting the decision the guards are empowered to dictate, because their action is for the good of the Unity.

In Our Own Words

Light and scent are our map of the world. Through either and both, we read Life Force and thus a map of the living world. At the moment each flower comes to its peak Life Force, the pollen and nectar are taken. Life Force holds within it the spiritual energies that convey themselves into us, and we eat and breathe them. The scent inhaled and ingested into us is every bit as important as the food itself.

Nutrition comes from food and also from the scent of a flower at peak readiness. Scent nurtures, heals and expands our bodies and our hive's consciousness. These collections of nectar and pollen invigorate us, stirring the hive's consciousness and expanding our being.

Within our hive, we build the Great Hall. Each hive builds its own hall and makes the interior of the hive a portal. Halls are created through the structure of the parallel combs and the hexagonal structures on them. The scent and sound within the hive is like a key within a keyhole. The way sound moves through the comb creates the keyhole sound. When the scent and sound are right, there is a transportation — like entering an elevator — that connects us with all other hives. We are all present in the experience of the other hives when we are in our halls. We feel all the joys and all the sufferings of all the other hives when they are in their halls.

The scenting we do when we enter a new hive — we atomize the air with our perfume, which induces a dreaminess in any who look our way. This provides a veil of obfuscation so those who gaze our way so they may look but will not see. Whereas the Queen scents individually to communicate to us, the maidens scent together to cloak us from outsiders.

Our scent induces a dreaminess, a forgetfulness even. It heightens the scent we send and calls attention not to us, but to one's interior. Those who look at us are slowly drawn to note how our scent affects them and, in that pause, as attention is drawn away from us and toward the other, the veil allows us to move freely within the shadow of the scent.

Each maiden bears a scent that describes her state of health. When a maiden reaches the end of her cycle, her scent, too, changes, and we know her end time is coming. Sometimes, we remove a bee early because we know her end is near. Once signaled, she will exit the hive and walk away. Thus the hive doesn't become cluttered with those who have passed.

Bees remove themselves by not returning home. They leave on their own once their end time becomes known to them. Even in their passing, they work for the good of the hive.

Anything within the hive that diminishes the hive's internal scent decreases bee health. In a weak hive the stench of disease drains our Life Force. Rather than remove the disease, we know to remove the bees. Despite human interventions, those bees, and therefore that hive, with rare exception, cannot achieve their fullest expression. Let the weakness die with the hive.

Some hives, if left alone, can remove the disease from their colony. Scent is the healer. This is why it is so important people not interfere. We have our own medicine. Some hives are capable of using the propolis in the manner it was designed, to heal itself.

We drink in the scent of our medicinals, the plants that heal us, the encapsulated light that gives us strength. Inhaling, drinking, drawing the scents into us strengthens our whole bodies and light moves through us where darkness had been. In this way a hive uses scent to bring about its own healing.

SOUND

"Constant Communication with All"

Bees don't have ears. You'd imagine they do, wouldn't you? Buzzing is certainly one of the qualities we associate with them. How curious then that sound, as we understand it, is not in their language. Yet if you go a little deeper and define sound as vibration, the bees have plenty to say.

When I first learned about the healing harmony of the songs the bees sing, the most powerful of which is called their "Song of Increase," I immediately thought that a solution to weak hives would be to play a strong hive sound to them. They would come into harmony with it, and all would be well. They do, after all, work on vibration.

The bees explained that when they are singing the Song of Increase, while it is about robust health, it is also about everything else that's going on in the hive. Every bee undertakes the appropriate action to move the Unity of the hive forward. In that song is the sound of the Queen laying her eggs, the maidens turning nectar into honey and the house bees repairing and making new wax. The drones are singing to the newborns, the house bees are producing fermented pollen and babies are coming to life in the nursery. The sound also communicates whether the ambient temperature needs to go up or down, the quality of the food in storage, and where help is needed for the tasks. These many sounds, all together, express everything happening throughout the hive.

What I came to understand is that the song conveys not just the sound of a strong hive, but also a full-on map of their home in this space and time. By being a part of the sound, a bee in one area can move to another knowing what task is occurring and if she is needed there for help.

For this reason, it's not useful to play the sound of a working hive to a weaker hive. In the weak hive the rooms don't exist that the sound describes and would lead to confusion. Like hearing someone else's memories playing in your head, they don't match with reality.

In Our Own Words

Our inner landscape is sound. We move between narrow paths and lanes and know the way by the resonance of sound as the waves move on to and off of every surface in the hive. Besides the information about the hive's activities moment to moment, the sound itself plays through the hive and describes the curves and contours of the internal shape of the hive. We see inside the hive by the shape of the sound, which is one more aspect of our Unity. In all our activities, we live inside the sound. Sound is integral in our Unity.

Sound is the emanation of our vibration. Each hive has a unique sound signature that declares its health and vital force. The emanation of the sound reinforces the state of health of the hive. It is as important as the warmth and scent of the hive.

Each bee individually has a sound declaring its health. In harmony together we setup a wave of sound that speaks (in a song) of hive health. The overlapping sounds harmonize on different frequencies that speak to each of the bee's organs. The song can raise or lower the vitality vibration, enhancing or decreasing hive health. Like a song of rapture, we can raise the spiritual song of the hive or, like an observation or complaint of ill health, it can wear it down.

Sound can heal bees by (1) directly templating the health pattern into our organs and immune systems; (2) uplifting the hive with a more vital vibration; and (3) Unifying us in the Song of Increase, which is the most joyful emanation our colony produces.

Each hive's sound describes that hive's health and status. Everything to be known about that hive is described in the sound. But this is not merely a telegraph of current conditions (though it is that). The sound is an emanation coming out from each individual in the hive, wrapped around and through each aspect of the hive. The effect of the sound as it vibrates through the structure also communicates something larger into the world.

In the world, there are healing chords that reverberate like tuning forks. These tones express love and they give, through their very structure, knowledge that continues the development and evolution of the world. Sound is the medium through which creation flows. The thought, "I am," spoken, becomes being and matter.

Throughout the world, sound sings our home into being. Places where there are loci of sound are especially vital — waterfalls, wind in trees, gamelin gongs and singing bowls, contented purring and laughter, the herd's thundering hooves, chattering insects and singing birds. Sound sings in native chanting, toning and drumming, in caverns and natural places where confined sound magnifies itself. Even the sound of a tornado or hurricane is a prayer as it washes clean the land and returns it to the fresh medium of silence upon which new can be written.

Thus sound is a returning place, a way of re-tuning ourselves to the original thought. Within the vibratory structure of a sound is the path to the matrix of matter. Returning to the sound recalibrates us, heals us, and allows transformation and evolution to the intended higher place.

Humans sing spirituals, chant, whistle, all with desire to heal, to impress the sound of their living and being upon the air.

The sound of the hive is healing. We sing the sound of our creation, a constant communication with 'all that is.' The sound of the hive tells everything about the health of the colony. The sound tells each bee what to do, where to be, how to engage. Each of the hive tasks are part of our sound. When all is right, the harmony is perfect.

Food made in such contentment nourishes our body and is balm for our soul. It is food made in prayer. Sugar syrup is too high pitched, like treacle. We eat it if we're hungry, but it makes our stomachs hurt, and it doesn't have the prayer in it. Sugar makes our singing weak and tinny. In almond orchards or places like this, we miss the natural world and suffer in our longing. We would benefit from beds of herbs planted where a tree has died out. We ask that you make garden beds and fill them with our medicine, flowering herbs.

In the hum of the hive, we see the hive entire. When we begin building, the imagination of our home already exists. We, in our industry, fill it in. When we visit a new home the first time, we enter and see our home hive already completed and filling the space. Our actions are simple: we see through our Unity's internal awareness, and from this we draw forth our imagination and express this into matter. We build ourselves from the inside out, from the thought to the matter.

THE SONG OF INCREASE

In the Unity of the hive, the flow of steady progress brings out the Song of Increase. A hive singing the Song of Increase is in full harmony. This is the highest state of being within the hive, the time when every bee is in right action and the hive is in full expression, when Love flourishes within the hive. This is what all hives seek, to sing the Song of Increase. This song nourishes bees by encouraging an expansive presence in each bee. Thus, we move within the hive with an emanation larger than our bodies, rippling off our hairs, which gives the impression that each bee glows, incandesces within the darkness of the hive.

Question: What would happen if a beekeeper introduced the sound of a healthy hive into a weaker hive? Would the weaker hive become stronger?

The intention is correct, but the application has an error. The sound of the healthy hive contains the tuning of good health and cooperation, which is good, but it also contains the map of comb and tasks that may not be appropriate for this hive. The sound of a hive tells that colony all that is happening within the hive. While the sound of the healthy hive could be helpful as a re-tuning, the 'furniture' of the healthy hive is also in that sound and would also be overlaid onto the weaker hive. The expression of the stronger hive will not match the structure of the weaker hive. The vibration of the sound is confirmed by the movement of the comb communicating the hive's activities saying, 'Here the Queen is laying eggs and over there we are packing pollen and here we are drawing down nectar and here we are shoring up with propolis the weave of wax.' These tasks would not match what the weak hive is doing in their hive.

What you intend by introducing the sound of good health is a right direction. The problem is that it contains too much specific information that will cause confusion in the weak hive's tasks.

A better sound would be taken from a new hive as it is set-
ting up housekeeping, a freshly started swarm. This new colony
is organized but still in the building state so the creative energy
is still being focused. They are drawing out the rooms from the
projected imagination. Thus a small hive may hear (by being im-
mersed in) the direction a strong hive is going. It may encourage
the bees to draw from within their own forces to be more.

But this cannot replace good genetics. It can only help if
the core strength is present but not fully awakened. Good genetics
are 100 percent necessary. A weak hive will eventually die off, and
this is appropriate.

For example — a secondary cast from a strong hive has
good genetics but may be hampered by small size. We need a vol-
ume of bees to build comb and feed everyone during the primary
construction. Otherwise the Queen will not have enough room to
lay eggs to increase the population. The continuing smallness of
the hive weighs on us. We seek a volume of sound around and
through the Unity that speaks of our success which encourages
more activity.

The simplest solution is to add brood from a healthy hive
and use the sound as support. Be watchful of the effects of the
sound and always be brief. Too much would cause harm.

This has not been done before, and we are wary of quick
solutions that do not address the underlying problems. Do not in-
troduce confusion. If the new sound riles, remove it. Listen to the
small hive while playing the new building sound a bit away from it.
If it creates stress, do not continue. If the smaller hive comes into
harmony with it, let it continue for no longer than two days. Then
diminish it so they can take up the sound themselves.

This is rocky ground because it is an artificial stimulation,
but it is appreciated that you seek to increase strength and vigor in
the weaker hives. Though a hive is weak, that does not mean it is

wrong. Weak hives also perform a service because they tell Nature that something is awry and out of balance. These hives give service as markers of imbalance. Their weakness is their service.

The underlying issues in Nature must be addressed to heal the bee family. Better actions are creating sanctuaries within the world, havens full of sound that involve Nature in every aspect. This is where true healing happens. Hives placed in such havens become stronger. This is the best direction through which to bring strength back into the hives and continue the evolution of the world.

QUANTUM MEASURE

"Beyond One to Oneness"

I've been in and out of hives hundreds, maybe thousands of times. Usually I have a reasonable expectation of what I'm going to see, but every so often the bees surprise me completely.

I use hives that don't have fixed frames inside them. In conventional beekeeping, the frames have four sides and a sheet of wax or plastic in the middle. The bees add their comb right onto the sheet and then fill it with nectar, pollen or larvae.

I try to do things more like bees do them in the wild so I use a simple top bar alone — just a strip of wood — and let the bees build the comb down in the way, size and shape they like. Usually it's pretty straight comb though sometimes in the vertical Warre hives it can be quite a maze because the bees build to retain heat and scent with no regard for where the top bars are. Sometimes their creations are architecturally exquisite.

A top bar hive is a bee-friendly hive that is long and horizontal, like a fallen log rather than a tall standing tree. The bees tend to build straight combs which makes them easier to work with. They start at the top of the wooden bar and build their pristine white comb down in an elliptical shape. If you pinned two pushpins to the top near the outside edges of the bar and then hung a thin gold chain between the pushpins, this would be the shape the bees create. Sometimes it's wide and the curve is long, other times it's narrower with a deeper pitch to the curve. Sometimes they will start two combs on either end of the same bar and, miracle of miracles, the two combs will join perfectly in the middle. I like to think my husband and I are well aligned in our shared vision, but I will readily admit that if he started building on one end of a wall and I started on the other, we are just not unified enough to have the wall meet neatly in the middle. Yet the bees, without measuring tools or math skills, do this perfectly and precisely every time.

Recently I read a scientist's article about bees in which the author — with great curiosity — stated that bees simply don't have a big enough brain to do all the things they do — and to do them so well — yet they do. Their unified intelligence is what science doesn't yet understand.

This brings me to my tale of gymnastic bees.

I had just hived a swarm and I usually give them a week or so to settle in undisturbed. A week later, I thought I'd peek in and see how they were doing. I opened the hive and removed a few top bars so I could look into the hive and, lo and behold, I saw a secret acrobatic performance.

A few hundred bees were latched arm to leg, hanging down from one of the bars in an amber-colored veil. They were suspended there, about fifty bees across and twenty-five bees down, strung like jewels in an intricate necklace of sequenced layers. Each bee held with her foreleg the hind leg of the bee above, all of them in matching rows. I was dumbfounded. What, what, what were they doing?

They were using their own bodies to place and measure how to build the comb. With their bodies, the bees measured out new comb. The maidens who construct the comb are given a mental picture of the completed comb through the action of these draftsman bees. Remembering that bees share a common consciousness, this system of measurement is constructed within the Unity's mind. This certainly stretches our understanding into quantum physics and that's a fair call. The bees use their bodies as measurement tools while the height, length, width, and pattern are conveyed to the comb-builders. Here, in their words, they explain bee measurement. Amazing.

In Our Own Words

We have a consciousness that extends beyond one to oneness.

When we hold our arms together in the open space, we are first building a template, spreading the measure of our bodies across the open space. It is as if we are standing upon the comb already built, as it exists in our perception. We see it there already and then we make it so.

The comb already IS in our consciousness and so we bring it to the present, as we first beheld it when the scouts saw it constructed within the space which we called home. The thought is expressed in love of one another. Upon the fabric of love it is writ.

When we hold the frame, we are moving between the work completed and the work as yet undone. These are simple steps and our work becomes manifestation. We bring forward what we imagine.

Herein we create a small part of the world without a single of us knowing naught more than the prescribed steps for one. But the one alone cannot bring even her part forward without the dreaming of the entire.

In the consciousness of the Unity, we build as one, both in space and time. We move freely between the place of imagining and the place of 'it is so.' The Unity moves between this natural fabric of time and matter.

Manifestation can be done, as humans sometimes do, using emotion as fuel but this can bring many entanglements that disrupt the clarity. We can also enliven our imaginations by all acting as one and in Unity which is simpler, cleaner. Thus the world we imagine becomes the world in which we live.

May you all live as one and build your home around the heart of your nature

PROPOLIS

"The Blood of the Trees"

In January after a few days of hard frost, I noticed that the bees who live in the upper wall of our farmhouse were particularly active. The air was still quite chilly, yet little clusters of bees excitedly scampered out their doorway and flew off in the cold sunshine. At first, I thought they were doing cleansing flights, hopping outside long enough to defecate and swooping back inside to the hive's self-generated warmth.

But no. These bees flew off toward the trees, and when they returned, their hind legs were covered with bright yellow pollen. Where in the world did they find flowers blooming in the brittle cold of winter?

I walked all over my farm looking for anything sprouting up from the frozen ground. Nothing. Buds on tree branches? How about blooming moss? Way too early. I was stretching and I just didn't see anything that looked like it was capable of providing pollen.

I positioned myself where I could see the bees exiting the hive, backlit by the sun's low rays. From underneath, I saw them silhouetted against the sky as they flew over the top of the roof to the front yard. I followed around to the other side of the house and watched until I saw the path they flew to a bushy ten-foot-tall hazelnut tree. Long clusters of golden brown catkins in full bloom were the center of each bee's attention.

Surprisingly, some flowers do bloom in winter — willow, witch hazel, hazelnuts. The pollen from these trees is particularly healthful to the bees, and on any warmish sunny day they will be all over their flowers. Sap also flows from some trees in late winter. On our farm, cottonwood, spruce and other evergreens contribute their sticky sap. The bees carry home winter sap, which they make into propolis, the source of the bees' medicine.

Propolis is a sticky, resinous substance of varied colors that bees create by mixing together tree and plant resins, beeswax, pollens, plus their own enzymes and glandular substances. The chemical and biochemical properties of propolis vary according to the bees collecting it, the collection areas, the time of year, and even the time of day. The propolis itself is an alchemical blend of hundreds of known and still unidentified biochemical processes.

While everyone has heard of honey and beeswax, many people are unaware of this other remarkable substance that is so much a part of the world of the honeybees. Bees make and use propolis to fulfill a wide variety of needs in colony life. Bees build propolis canals on the walls and ceilings of their hives to move the condensation water that comes from both the high interior hive temperatures and the evaporation process that turns flower nectar into honey. This water is directed away from the combs and allowed to pool in certain places so that bees can have a drink of water without having to leave the hive.

Hive walls and surfaces are coated in thin skins of propolis that "weather strip" cracks inside the hive where drafts may enter. The propolis itself is waterproof, helping to maintain the critical hive humidity level of 90-percent-plus that is crucial to healthy brood. Many viruses, certain bacteria and mites cannot survive in such a hot and humid environment. This is only one of the many ways propolis protects the health of the colony.

Conversely, many other bacteria and yeast thrive in such a damp and dark environment and could endanger the colony if unchecked. In direct response to this, propolis is known to have powerful antimicrobial, antifungal and antibacterial properties. Aromatically, the propolis releases strong resin and essential oil scents that kill off specific organisms harmful to bees. This same scent is also a healing balm and immune stimulant to bees, who have little internal immune defenses. Propolis is, in effect, the external immune body of the bee.

I'm quite fond of this observation from Dr. Peter Mansfield, the founder of Good Health Keeping in England. He uses propolis in his medical practice and has this to say about it, as quoted in *Bee Propolis: Natural Healing from the Hive* by James Fearnley:

"Some of its properties defy not just chemical analysis but the very principles of chemistry. The interior of the beehive is a remarkably clean place, sterile place — far more so than the surgical departments of most hospitals. Yet this is achieved not by dosing all the bees individually, nor by lining the entire honeycomb, but by an outer skin of propolis alone."

In the same book, these words from James Fearnley:

"The beehive is a symbol of how simpler substances derived from the lower order of the plant world are elevated and transformed by the bee into substances appropriate for a higher order of existence."

Bees paint their comb with propolis to sterilize the cells for the pips. They use propolis to stabilize the wax so that it is better able to carry the full weight of matured honey. Propolis is used at hive entrances to open or reduce the entrance. In fall when the days are variably warm or cold, I've seen the entrance modified daily. They use propolis to create narrow tubes the bees pass through when arriving and leaving the hive entrance. These reduced entrances are easier for the guard bees to protect from intruders and also serve as decontamination chambers for bees who have been out in the world and may have brought something harmful back with them.

When bees have been domesticated for many generations, they sometimes lose skills and abilities that feral bees still attend to. The bees on our farm are all from feral stock and most are adept at modifying their front entrance to fit their seasonal needs. One hive in particular changes their entrance as often as once or twice a week. They built a scrim of propolis just inside the wider entrance and, from here, they can limit access to prevent robbing, increase or reduce ventilation and moisture, stave off cold winds, or fling the doors open to let the multitudes of foragers in and out during peak nectar flows.

Closed, the scrim has an opening only as wide as two bees, a common situation in winter. I've seen other hives seal the door nearly shut when yellow jackets tried to storm the entrance. Other times the bees may open up multiple doors within the scrim. If I suspect the hive needs better ventilation, I may give the bees a hive box or super with a small round opening on the back side. They leave it open when they want to move the inner air more efficiently and they close it off when that's no longer needed.

Propolis can be used to seal over anything the bees can't carry out. A friend was doing a hive inspection in early spring and reported that she discovered a large lump of propolis as big as her thumb in a lower corner. She cut the lump out and found inside a dried up mouse body. Apparently the mouse found the hive a warm and inviting place to build a nest for winter and set up housekeeping in the corner. The bees, of course, wanted nothing to do with a smelly mouse who would pee and poop in their immaculate home so they sealed the mouse into a propolized sarcophagus, thus safely entombing and mummifying the intruder.

The bees tell me of the healing properties of the propolis, and describe the aroma as a kind of vibratory signature. Each hive in their unique location crafts a distinctive type of propolis that may differ from the recipes of its neighbor. This finely crafted substance is the exact medicine needed to combat the weaknesses of that singular hive in that particular area. I see the uniqueness of my local region in the scarlet red propolis bees on our farm create. A few miles away and at a different elevation, a good friend's bees make butterscotch colored propolis with an entirely different scent.

On our farm, we do our best to keep the environment vibrantly healthy for bees. Our intention is to give them many different ways to stay in good health including a wide variety of seasonal plantings of herbs and flowers that let them choose their own medicines, especially borage, flax, and thyme. At the edge of our garden irrigation we have a pile of seaweed that gets a sprinkling each morning at dawn to keep it from drying out. I often find them lined up on the edge of a seaweed puddle, sipping with their hollow tongues that work like straws. The sea water gives them access to the full range of trace minerals that bees might need. My friend Glenna puts a handful of oyster shell chips in her watering station and she says they like that, too.

Much of my work with bees takes place outside the hive where I do my best to give them the proper environment to provide for their own health. I trust the bee teachings and the wisdom of treatment-free beekeeping. Nature wants strong genes in the gene pool so I let weak hives die and have confidence that the stronger hives will survive, improving the gene pool as they do. To that end, I don't treat with chemicals, medications or even natural products. Instead our farm has many trees and plants that provide good nutrition and ingredients for them to make their own medicine: propolis.

Letting Nature take its course is a long and sometimes painful path for a beekeeper to walk. I believe this is how bees direct themselves toward self-preservation. They will survive if we can keep our fingers off them long enough to let them bring forth processes that are already present in the collective mind of their knowledge and to develop new natural systems.

A few years ago we inadvertently brought a colony with deformed wing virus (DWV) into our bee yard. Mites lay their eggs in the cells of unborn pips so that when the baby bee is born, it comes out into the world already covered with blood-sucking mites that weaken the bee as it matures. Mites can be devastating on their own but even more so when the mites carry the virus and infect the pips with it. The virus prevents their wings from forming correctly. Without wings, bees can't fly out to the flower fields. No wings, no foragers.

Swarming is Nature's way to break a disease cycle. When the swarm moves into a new home, that new home will not yet have any cells for the mites to infest because the bees haven't yet started constructing the brood chamber. The bees will start building new comb but it takes awhile to be ready for the Queen to start laying eggs, long enough to throw the mites out of synch with the brood's hatch cycle. This effectively puts the mites out of business. Yet conventional beekeeping thwarts swarming and does its best to prevent this magnificent and health-giving event from occurring. If they only knew how beneficial it is to the bees!

After a colony swarms and moves into their new home, the mites have nowhere to lay their eggs. Hopefully this brief phase is long enough to cause the old mites to die off. When you allow swarming, Nature interrupts the mite life cycle and gives the bees a fresh start. When beekeepers forbid swarming, they also prevent the bees from ridding themselves of the pest.

The colony I had collected wasn't a swarm. A barn owner had asked us to remove them from the structure's wall. I didn't know they had mites and, during the transfer, I placed much of their mite-infested brood comb in the new hive. Soon after this colony arrived, I saw bees at the front entrance with mites on their bodies and realized what I'd done.

First I had to teach myself not to worry about them. Worrying about the bees doesn't change anything, it just increases stress for everyone. Instead I prayed these bees would become the healthiest they could be. I blessed them with good thoughts and let them handle their own recovery. I am not saying I just walked away. I stayed connected with the colony through prayer which was part of my own education about how to support the bees.

In past situations the bees had been able to tell when I was upset and gave me feedback in the form of a warning sting. When I hadn't been in the right place in my thinking, they told me to stay away. The next step for me was to realize they could also perceive when I am caring for and loving around them.

So I put my thoughts to imagining them strong and healthy, a vibrant hive capable of surmounting any odds and becoming robust again. I resisted the urge to open the hive and check on them, instead monitoring the entrance to gauge how they were faring.

The sanctity of the hive is precious when bees are dealing with a disease process. These bees needed to seal their home so they could begin their healing. How the bees keep the hive sealed is especially important and ensures their access to all the benefits of the propolis, especially in the hive air. It's my belief that they build strength through maintaining a sealed environment.

I could tell the bees were improving week by week. They began their healing process by removing from the hive any mature bees with the tell-tale shriveled wings. Next they went into the cells and began taking out infected larvae. They were thorough and dedicated. When I saw them pulling infested pips out, I knew they were going to make it. The entire process took about ten or twelve weeks. At the end of it, the bees were mite-free, once again strong and robustly healthy and have continued on that way.

I believe bees who heal in this way are propagating an appropriate self-generated response to a disease, expressing their willingness and ability to deal with it. They clean up anything associated with the virus and eventually are either free of the mites or they have arrived at a comfortable symbiotic relationship wherein they are not overrun or debilitated by the mites being present in a small quantity.

I have been sharing what propolis means to the life of the hive, but propolis also has a long history with human healing. For thousands of years, teachers and healers from Hippocrates to Aristotle wrote of the medicinal qualities of honey, propolis and beeswax. In further chapters we will explore how to use propolis for healing. But for now, it is enough to know of yet one more wondrous creation from the humble and generous bee.

In Our Own Words

Propolis comes from the trees. Sap is the blood of the trees. We are, as you would call it, chemists or, more appropriately, alchemists who create our own medicines. This is not a random mix. We know when we have enough of one and need more of another. The resins release powerful scents into the air and all around us. We live inside the envelope of our medicine. Bees seek to live in hollow trees because the natural oils of the trees will be combined into the propolis recipe, which is aligned with the living system of bees and other beings. Propolis sorts the negative from the positive life-supporting organisms and conditions.

Imagine your home if you lived within the holy space of constant and ongoing healing, surrounded by scents and sounds that continually bring you to more of your self. You might ask, 'Does this sound enrich me into expanding consciousness? Does what I breathe into my body bring health and wisdom?'

The structure of propolis has different keys that fill our damaged places and stimulate the limbic system to draw off the poison by wrapping it with a woven blanket of frequencies that deter, disable or dissemble its course. The scents have frequencies that render the invading process to nil. Humans have undervalued the power of scent and sound. The frequencies contained in propolis latch onto the imbalance and bring it again to equilibrium.

Health is calibrated inside a narrow frame. The stronger we are, the broader the frame. Weakened bees are precariously balanced with little room for damage.

Just as we need many sources of flowers, we must also have a forest with wide ranges of trees. The trees freely share their lifeblood and, thus, they too are valued healers. We are as strong as our surroundings. Propolis is best made from many sources

— some even quite small — so we can heal whatever ails us. The trees and flowers contribute to our good health, and we revel in their gifts and generosity. We revel, too, in the propolis air and our Queen's glorious fragrance that surrounds us.

A wild hive is sealed with propolis where air enters or escapes. Breaking the seal opens the hive to outer influences that are hard to control. The propolis seal is meant to be near inviolable. When humans break the seal, we can repair it but it draws energy away from progress. The flow of steady progress is a balm to us. When humans pull apart a hive to see what is happening inside, the healing medicinal air is dissipated, diluting its beneficial effects. By sealing the air, we control our environment and retain the maximum benefits of this universal healing substance.

We encourage you to breathe the mixed scents of propolis. It will bring you to clear thinking, yet another aspect of good health.

DEFENSE

"A Challenge of Unification"

Late in swarm season, about midsummer and well after most colonies had swarmed, I got a call to pick up a softball-sized swarm hanging in a tree. Because of their late start, this swarm had half as many bees as an early season swarm. They had fewer bees to help out which meant they would be hard pressed to complete all their tasks by fall and be ready for winter. But I have a soft spot in my heart for swarms, big or small, so I brought them home and gave them their own hive.

All through the rest of July and into August, they toiled away making fresh comb and filling it with brood, nectar and pollen. Small as the colony was, it looked like they might, with a little bit of luck and good weather, increase their population and put enough away for winter.

Ever the optimist, I hoped my positive opinion might encourage them. I hoped the colony was big enough to make it through the winter. My common sense, however, told me they just didn't have enough bees to make a large cluster to keep them snug and warm in the cold months.

In late August I noticed a flurry of activity outside their hive with many bees in the air. My first thought was that this was the hatch of a population surge and these were young bees doing their first flights.

"Hurrah! With this many bees they'll make it," I thought. But, as I got closer, I saw details that told me the fates weren't tipping in their favor. The most telling clue was the struggle at the front door as guard bees fought to defend the entrance and keep outsiders from getting inside and stealing their honey. The hive's guard bees were wrapped in leg-to-leg combat, stinging interlopers and fighting as hard as they could to keep the marauders from sneaking inside. The aggressor bees were flying wave after wave of advancing troops at the little hive's entrance.

Foraging bees normally come back from the fields loaded with nectar. Bees with a full load come in with their feet dangling forward in a tuck as they jockey for a landing spot. Robber bees also hang in the air as they search for a landing spot, but they're coming in empty so their bodies are more elongated and their legs hang out behind them. The cloud of bees in front of the hive was coming in empty, hoping to rob what they could inside and then depart with a full belly back to their home hive.

Robbing, once started, is difficult to stop because the robbers have had a taste of what's inside. When we see robbing in our bee yard, we place homemade robber screens in front of the entrance. These screens complicate the entrance, which sometimes foils the robbers who then depart. We also put leafy branches in front of the entrance to make it more difficult for the robbers to find the entrance and easier for the guard bees to defend it.

I knew the hive was weak and the fact the hive was being robbed confirmed it. I put the robber screen up and waved a bunch of robbers away, but I knew this hive was not likely to survive and that made me sad. I had given them the best chance I could, even helping them during the attack, but the robbers were too strong and the little hive too weak. A day later they succumbed.

With this loss fresh in my mind, I asked why this happened, why this hive had to die and why other hives who seem to start off strong ended up failing, too. In my thoughts I wondered about mites and robbers and all the ways that a perfectly good hive comes to an end.

The Overlighting Being

Mites are not the bad guys. Mites cull weakness out of the hive. Each divine bee being has a gauntlet to run, something that asks or tests him or her. It may be the endurance of a long forage line, or the task of bearing up the measure of a comb length, or the frost initiating the call for extreme heat. Healthy bees meet each challenge and the hive thrives.

When something is not right within the hive, the bees become distracted from the template of their tasks. Their sound goes off, like when they can't find their Queen, and a keynote of distraction enters their song. They begin to sing, 'We are doing the best we can,' instead of 'All is well in the world.' It is a song that addresses a weakness they know is present, and often a painful distraction. These distractions can be large or small, the song will always tell where the hive stands in relation to the challenge.

A challenge from without, like yellow jackets or robber bees attacking the colony, mobilizes the hive to defense, and a strong sharp note presses out of them. This is the 'Territory Song,'

145

a defensive wall of sound, which pushes out the entrance and lays claim to the hive's territory. The defensive song emanates from all the bees inside the hive, bolstering the defenders of the hive — the guard bees — who know the hive is in full consciousness of their mission to protect the hive.

Likewise robber bees have a Song of Assertion. Always the challenge is to cull out weakness, and robber bees are in service to the culling in the bee community. If won, the attack culls the weaker hive, and the stolen plunder from the weaker hive increases the stores of the robbing hive.

Before the attack, the defensive hive had tried continually to move itself to strength and harmony. If the hive is below par, the disturbances they experience — too few foragers, not enough comb being made, insufficient pollen — all draw attention away from the regularity of the hive's tasks. They respond with less solidarity and ultimately fail.

In most situations, the home hive has the advantage and if they are able to maintain their cohesiveness, they easily throw off the challenge. Survival comes if the hive defends properly and the robbers withdraw.

This test is a challenge of unification. The timing is precise; the bees must respond in an instant and cannot be distracted. They need the ability to shift the efficacy of purpose to meet the challenge. This is a test of timing, punctuality, response to an alarm. When a challenge comes from within, the hive draws strength from stability.

At every moment each bee has a single-minded purpose. The attack calls on the ability of the bees to shift, to know what next needs to be done. The hive depends on the unified body always knowing what is needed in that moment.

A ROBBING TALE

In any endeavor, it is normal to want to do and to know the right thing. It is natural to want to know all about what you are doing, so you can more confidently predict a good outcome. But beekeeping is confounding in this way because bees don't always act according to plan, or common wisdom or anything else you might imagine.

You will already have noticed that one of the tenets of the way I practice keeping bees is to be quite hands off. However, there is one situation that I get very hands on about: robbing. Sometimes robbing happens when the weather has worked against the bees, as when a drought dries up all the bloom or too much rain has depleted the flowers of nectar and pollen and shortened the season. In such a situation, the bees are stressed and may get desperate to increase their stores by robbing any hives they can find. The robbers may be honeybees or they may be yellow jackets. In either case, the victimized hive may lose everything they've put aside for winter and — even if they were once strong — become weak or die completely. I do protect my hives from robbing.

My friend Tel gave me a hive I call the Sunshine Hive. I noticed in midsummer this hive was being attacked by robber bees. I minimized the entrance on the hive so the guard bees could protect it better. I suspected a nearby hive, called the South Hive, was doing the robbing as the amount of activity at the Sunshine Hive entrance matched precisely the activity at the South Hive entrance. These days I have robber screens that prevent this but at the time I didn't know about such things.

The Sunshine Hive entrance was less than an inch. At this width only one bee at a time could enter or leave through the door, a situation that gave the guard bees a better chance to keep the interlopers out. Even so, the South bees relentlessly rushed it all morning. Finally at midday, and in frustration, I put a screen across the entire entrance and told them everyone had to stay where they were, in or out, and that I'd open the screen at dusk to let everyone go back to their proper hive. Normally I wouldn't screen a hive in the hot summer sun because the interior of the hive would lose its ventilation and get too hot, but the South Hive was well-shaded and cool.

I once heard a curious tale that said when closed in together, robber bees may become acclimated to the bees in the hive they are robbing and the robbers may switch camps. I opened the hive at dusk, and some bees rushed out but there was no flurry and everything was much calmer. I kept an eye on this hive, and the next day the robbing ceased.

In the meantime, I noticed something unusual at the South Hive. I spent plenty of time watching them through the observation window and was familiar with their normal busy pace, but they seemed to be aimlessly wandering as if they were looking for something and were not as active. I wondered if they might be Queen-less.

When you spend time watching your hives and being involved with them or in them, you learn about your bees. You learn each hive's unique personality — every hive is different — and you learn to recognize when something is "off." There are ways of being with bees that are respectful and that don't impede the daily business of the hive. I make sure to listen to my bees so that if they are having an off day, they can let me know in little, gentle ways short of a sting. Because I'd been so involved with both these hives for a few years, I knew something was up, and made sure to be especially watchful after the robbing incident. My instincts paid off, and I was able to be present for and witness a rather remarkable event in my bee yard.

I woke up at dawn to watch, before any bees had left their own hives, because the behavior of the South Hive didn't make sense to me. Through the observation window, I watched the South bees load up with honey and, earlier than any other hives were active, leave out the front door. The Sunshine hive had no activity yet, but the South bees were already up. They were moving everything over to the Sunshine Hive. I saw, with my own eyes, the South bees pillage their own stores and with heavy loads, head over to the Sunshine Hive and enter. The South bees were flying with full bellies, their legs unmistakably dangling forward. The Sunshine Hive guard bees seemed to recognize them and waved them right inside. It was robbing, in reverse.

Over the next day and a half all the South bees migrated into the Sunshine Hive. My guess was something bad happened to the South Queen and, instead of the hive slowly dying off, they pitched their lot in together with another successful hive and made a go of it.

The Sunshine Hive is particularly generous in making others feel welcome. Weeks earlier, I found a small pod of scout bees who missed catching up with their swarm. Not knowing what to

149

do with them (rain was coming), I put them into a small hive body but I knew the little queenless cluster wasn't big enough to make it on their own. A few days later I decided to merge them with the Sunshine Hive. Instead of letting them do a gradual introduction, my intuition said to try something different.

I inched the hive cover back, exposing two bars. That way I didn't alarm the Sunshine Hive, and I could easily see if this would work or not. Then I gently dropped handfuls of the stray bees at this opening. I was curious whether the home hive would try to exclude them. If so, I would have stopped.

When these first few abandoned bees made contact, there was a lot of touching and checking them out. When the home bees walked back to their tasks, this little crew of bees slipped into the hive and I felt sure I could see them grinning, like sailors lost at sea who'd suddenly found land. Such good fortune! The new bees immediately got to work helping. They integrated in just a few minutes and everyone went back to work. I have marveled at how welcoming this hive has been, twice now.

Tel came over to open the empty hive with me and see if we could figure out what happened. We started pulling combs out and saw what happened. The hive had a summer's worth of honey. In the brood chamber, however, we found not a single maiden egg. Plenty of drone brood was spread about, some of it already hatched, but no maidens. That told me the Queen was gone.

When a Queen is injured or her fertility declines, the colony quickly replaces her. The brood chamber bees choose a new maiden cell in the middle of the comb, and they quickly alter the size and shape to turn that tiny pip's cell into a Queen cell. Instead of pollen, they feed her royal jelly and the pip that had been on her way to becoming a maiden instead becomes a Queen.

As expected, I found a queen cell right in the middle of a sheet of comb. The fully developed cell had a round hole in the bottom which told me she'd grown to maturity and hatched out. Once hatched, she left the hive for a mating flight, and something must have happened. Being midsummer, there were still plenty of drones around so my best guess was that a bird ate her on the way home to the hive.

The new queen hadn't returned, and there were no young eggs ready to turn into another new queen. Knowing the hive's days were numbered, one of the maidens stepped forward and volunteered to be a stand-in Queen. Being unfertilized, she was only able to lay infertile eggs which become drones. The nurse bees waited till the drone eggs were ready to hatch. Meanwhile the South Hive established a relationship with the Sunshine Hive and, on an appointed day, they moved their honey and the rest of their family over there, leaving the nursery unattended and empty.

I had been told a Queen-less hive who doesn't create a new queen simply dies off. At best, a drone-laying maiden might step forward and produce drone eggs but, after that last task, the entire hive predictably dwindles and dies.

Except in this case. What do you do when you see behavior that flies in the face of common knowledge? I am in a beekeeping group run by my bee friend from Wales, David Heaf. David is also an open-minded scientist and I thoroughly enjoy our conversations. I sent off the details asking if he or anyone in the group had ever seen such a thing. David found this explanation of silent robbing in the Illustrated Encyclopaedia of Beekeeping by Morse & Hooper:

"Silent robbing occurs when robbing has reached a state where the two colonies are completely friendly with each other, and the robbers are going in and out of the hives amongst the rightful owners without being molested by guards...The usual outcome of this situation is that the bees all finish up in one hive."

Unexpected compassion. That's what I saw.

THE SONG
OF
INCREASE

IV

"The Song of the World"

A hive contains thirty to fifty-thousand bees. Of these bees, about a third are the foraging maidens. These are the bees who go out into the world, the bees we meet on flowers in our gardens. Drones are busy seeking out virgin queens, and we rarely encounter them in our yards or meadows.

It is this foraging maiden who ventures out into the world of wind, flowers and light. Most of what is known about foraging bees has to do with pollen and nectar collection activities. After all, this looks like what they are doing as they visit thousands of flowers each day, and it is part of what they are doing.

But there is more, so much more. The bees have shared a wondrous, epic story of mineral migration, planetary ethers, light layering, faeries and gnomes, and memory made into physical matter. Many of these messages from the bees are supported by new and ever-more mind-boggling research on honeybees and their extraordinary world.

We understand bees collect nectar and pollinate flowers, but as the bees explain, they endeavor to collect only the very best nectar and pollen from the healthiest of flowers. These must be collected at specific times of the day and at specific developmental stages of the flowering plant. It is also their task to see that these prime plant specimens are able to advance and thrive in accordance with the will and divine directive of the minerals and soil within their Bien.

Bees are exemplars of communication with their own kind as well as with beings among all Creation. How do they do this? And what can we learn from them? In this chapter, we will follow the foraging maiden out into her world.

THE COMMUNION OF BEES & FLOWERS

"Libraries of Honey & Pollen"

I grew up in a small New England town on country land with orchards, wetlands, pastures, hillsides, woodlands, and a pond. At a precociously early age I knew the names, whereabouts and bloom times of all the plants in our area. I noticed, too, how some plants were fixed in their locations, like the white trilliums that rose from the same root each spring, while asters and golden-rod seemed to wander a bit. I watched yellow pond lilies thrive in our pond for many years, then something changed and a surge of purple pickerelweed nearly replaced the pond lilies.

To this day, I find great satisfaction in knowing the flora of my area and what blooms where and when. I have been influenced by the intriguing writings of philosopher-scientist Rudolf Steiner and the principles of biodynamic farming we use here on our land. Add to that my direct communication with bees and it's probably no surprise I have a broader expectation of what bees are doing when they pollinate flowers.

I am in full accord with Steiner's belief that the earth is populated with a wide variety of helpful nature spirits, including the realms of faerie beings, which I sense in the Life Force present in different areas of our farm. It follows that I believe bees partner closely — to the point of what we might call communion — with the plant spirits or beings.

The plants themselves are the emissaries, co-partners, and feet — if you will — for the mineral kingdom, the realm of the gnomes. According to Steiner, the mineral kingdom has a mission and purpose of its own: the minerals strive to create balance and harmony across the earth. They do their work slowly, over eons of time, moving too subtly to be seen or felt by humans but are explicitly noticed by nature spirits, plants and bees. Plant and tree roots draw minerals up and carry the news of each mineral's presence to the air spirits and the insects. The insects can move minerals by eating the plant, moving elsewhere and dying leaving their mineral-laden carcasses behind. Even though it seems small, a lot of mineral movement is achieved this way though not with what we would call speed. There is no hurry when time is measured in epochs.

Plants flourish or fail as they wander across the landscape. They follow the directive of the mineral realms which determine the soil components that feed each kind of plant. Wild blueberry bushes may thrive in one area for a century, roots happily ensconced in their desired blend of minerals. These particular minerals may eventually peter out and give rise to a different kind of soil. Then the blueberries will grow more slowly, bear less fruit, and in their weakness they become susceptible to diseases and die out, to be replaced by another plant who finds that combination of minerals and soil perfect. In great part, the minerals influence soil life, and that determines the health of the plants and trees that grow there.

Some plants, like dandelions and comfrey, act as miners who burrow far into the ground where certain minerals live. Dandelion's deep taproot finds calcium, iron, and other minerals and raises them to the surface via their leaves, flowers and shallower roots. When they die back and decompose the mineral-rich leaves and flowers are deposited on the surface, changing the mineral composition of that land.

I've seen this in our own yard. A dozen years ago the front yard was a riot of smiling yellow dandelion faces each spring. Over the years we have encouraged the dandelions to complete their task by letting them stay and not trying to remove or deter them. As these plants died their bodies became mineral bundles in themselves, further feeding the soil and fully transforming the landscape over time. A dozen years later we see they have brought enough calcium to the surface that the soil there no longer needs their care and the dandelions have diminished significantly. Apparently now our north yard has need of their skills so they have begun to move there.

Across the land, many plants participate in accessing and moving minerals. The job of each weed is to determine what is missing from the soils in that area and then try its best to create balance. That could mean mining minerals, creating vitamin-rich mulch or significantly loosening up the soil structure so other plants can follow. Weeds work hard to accumulate the nutrients needed to make the soil more balanced.

What role do bees play in this? More than you can imagine. The flowers need to know where to move to next, and the bees convey that information and more. Every speck of pollen is a collection of knowledge about the plant, where it came from and its connection to the mineral world around it. Bees perceive with their senses the unique chemical, nutrient and mineral stamp of each plant. They understand this information as a language: the language of plants and minerals. This deep consciousness that passes between the bees and the flowers is a crucial aspect of pollination that far surpasses the simple fertilization we imagine.

In the act of pollination, bees are performing two crucial tasks. First, they move the buds of pollen from flower to flower. These pollens contain information of past, present and future mineral migration and the bees spread this knowledge between individual plants. Second, the bees impart an energetic stamp of awareness and approval onto each flower and that is crucial to the evolution of plants. This energy stamp, or transfer of consciousness between plant and bee, both begins and completes the plant's awareness of itself as a singular plant that is also part of the unity of plants in its family.

Each cluster of bees daily finds and connects with the etheric communication between plants. Each group of bees works only with one type of plant for that particular foraging trip and perhaps many foraging trips that day. A single bee can visit over 500 plants in one foraging excursion and can make more than thirty foraging trips a day. Flowers species are, for the most part, not mingled on pollination journeys. This allows for a more robust imprinting of the information that is to be shared among that plant family.

The bees also know which plants are the strongest, and these are the ones they visit, moving the healthiest pollens across the landscape. I see this in my own gardens. When we first moved here I planted a garden in the front yard that I didn't amend well. It has been on my to-do list for a while to add richer soil and help those plants along. I have autumn-blooming sedums growing there and in other places around the farm including some beds where the soil is near ideal for those plants. In fall, the bees visit all the sedums, but they visit the flowers in the better beds three times as often. Even I can see the differences in the pale front yard plants and the more robust and deeply colored plants in the other beds.

Much of our garden beds have been tended, as humans do, with volitional plantings. I want the plants to be healthy but, rather than planting only what would grow best in our unamended soil, we loosened up the earth and added minerals that make the beds appropriate for the fruit, vegetables, and flowers we plant into them. By properly amending I can coax the soil into being more readily perfect, even for plants foreign to my area.

This task of amending would take far longer if left to Nature. There is a major difference in my garden, however. It has to be cared for by a human. If I ever stopped gardening, the land would revert to woodland and, ultimately, to forest, in less than a decade. My method is not sustainable without my human input. In Nature, the process moves slowly but efficiently. Wild flowers bloom in the shadow of big trees, swamps nurture wetland willows and cattails, and sun- drenched flower fields walk across the land in the wake of wildfires and avalanches.

As bees gather nectar and pollen, they deeply sense the history of the land. They understand the intent, through the pollen and nectar, to expand the movement of plants to their rightful places. Even in my beds where the plants are well contained, I notice differences in how the bees treat them and the effects of those visits. The most robust plants get more bee visits, and the increased visitations seem to make the healthy plants healthier. The more vigorous plants multiply faster and are ready to expand into larger territory.

As a gardener, I have a responsibility to listen and respond to these plants so I, too, am included in this conversation. Until I paid attention, I hadn't realized my edged beds restrained their desire to expand, and I bet that was frustrating for them. Now that I understand the communication, I comply. Plants this healthy need to expand. Taking a signal from that, I dedicate more places to them where they can do what they intend. That's the best I can do as a human.

Now we're going to look at how the bees participate in plant migrations. While I can add minerals and plant seeds, bees assist in a deeper, more sacred way. In their awareness of a plant's history they provide a mysterious and crucial service by witnessing and acknowledging the essential presence of the plants. (Please don't skim over that sentence. Back up and read it again.)

In physics we read about the capacity of the observer to change the observed: witnessing and remembering are powerful, little-understood, cosmic acts or forces. As the bees move from flower to flower, bringing their witnessing power to bear, a jolt of Life Force is injected into the plant each time they interact with it. The bees tell me that this brings a "trembling delight to the plant beings, and creates JOY throughout Nature."

As the bees begin speaking on this topic, they mention they work to 'revitalize the ether.' Since 'ether' isn't a word I normally use, I looked up the meaning. I had a smile on my face as I read the Oxford dictionary definition: "a very rarefied and highly elastic substance formerly believed to permeate all space, including the interstices between the particles of matter, and to be the medium whose vibrations constituted light and other electromagnetic radiation."

In Our Own Words

Pollination is so much more than cross-fertilization. Pollination is as much about moving the reproductive forces as it is about enlivening the ether. Both are important and they happen as the pause between beats in music amplifies and describes the rhythm itself. Pollinating and the daily revitalizing of the ether is our task. We are embedded into the task as it is in us, and we have no singularity of it.

THE SONG OF INCREASE

The trails we leave in the ether are webs of protection over the Earth. Each distance we travel between hive and flower is enlivened. That's why we travel so far, because a closer distance would leave gaps, holes in the natural world. We enliven the green world. It is our charge.

Honey contains all the minerals needed for good health. Each mineral has a sound signature that creates harmony within the being who eats that honey. The designs of the flowers, their shape and structure, are part of the vibrational emanation. The world is so much vaster than humans imagine.

These songs are always being sung. These clusters of blooming color, effusing scent, and rising sound are all communications between Life constantly emerging in a cohesive, eternal collaboration that creates Life and more Life. All pollinators participate in some way. Honeybees, though, bring the spark of consciousness, of unity, and love as they do their task and thus work presciently into the future to bring the heartful presence of love into the world.

We are the bearers of the energy stamp of Creation. The bee's exhalation infuses this energy stamp into the plant. The moistness is a trigger that wakes up the plant and announces the energy transfer which the flower receives and acknowledges. Flowers are completed when the pollens are delivered. Each flower is fulfilled as it receives our encoded transfer. The flowers thus communicate through their pollination that they are in unison, bringing forth the same WORD.

Each colony has a significant role to play in the area where it lives, reacquainting the hive with the local plants and the geological architecture through the seasons and through the decades and centuries as the minerals reveal themselves in their slow migration across the land's surface. Bees are meant to be in their own areas. When humans move us, that compendium of local knowledge is shattered and lost.

The mineral story is told by the flowers and then communicated across the landscape by the trails of bees in flight, and ultimately held in our libraries of honey and pollen. The ordering within the libraries is by chronology. The flow of seasons ripples across the comb, down the long sheet, much like a calendar. The flowers poured themselves into each drop of nectar. Thus we know the minerals they shared and we stored.

During the winter vision time when we eat the honeys made during different times of year, we are memory keepers of the flowers. These honey stories tell the history of the plants and the land's geological shifts. They contain the directive for the future of the plants and minerals, telling where they are heading. In this way, bees and the winter-dormant plants remain vibrant to each other and keep alive the energetic Unity of bee and plant.

Imagine you found a book along a trail that says, 'Herein lies our history. The lands from which we have come; the places we have stayed along our way and what each time in those places has done with us.' The book describes generations of great expansion, advancing into new areas, how the plant family flourished. And there are stories of great difficulty, of weather and dearth of needed minerals. They tell the paucity of the days, the struggle to thrive and sometimes a retreat when the minerals gave out in that area and the plants moved elsewhere. Mingled in the nectar and pollen we consume is our own contribution to the history of the plants.

We read this history from the groupings of nectars. They tell us how whole seasons unfolded, the diverse plants in sequence and their relationships to each other in the mineral blends and mineral fields. We are particularly attuned to awareness of mineral presences throughout the land.

We don't read the maps of minerals like humans pore over maps to plan a trip, choosing on a whim where they'll next go. The knowledge in these historical and geological maps allows us to be present to a flow of information which already contains the route the landscape will take. We read and know in the same instant, an emerging awareness of mineral knowledge in its own slow movement delineating a path already laid in and through time.

The mineral map can be altered by subtle geological shifts as the land moves, opening and closing veins and mingling ores. Wind and birds spread seeds, ferns and horsetail arrive, mosses and primitive plants expand to cover and protect the exposed land, holding moisture so the reclamation plants can establish. Thus new lands open.

Humans, however, greatly alter terrains, and these sudden shifts require much attention from the plant community to bring that land into balance again. Whole plant families rush in to disturbed areas to begin balancing what has been undone. When the land becomes too barren, greater forces come present and move minerals in a far larger manner by letting the seawaters wash over the lands. Thus minerals are replenished in broad areas so we can begin anew.

Monocultures are deserts. They are mistaken notions of the purpose of plants. Monocultures thwart the progress of mineral knowledge between plant families and the progress and transfer of mineral migration. Instead, altered mineral combinations are dumped into areas and weed suppression begins. Although humans decide a certain kind of plant should grow there, little attention is given to the many minerals those plants most desire to thrive. Neglecting this makes the plants weak.

We try to help by conveying this information to the flowers, but there are few nearby tracts of land for the necessary healing weeds to volunteer from. Areas of low diversity are an anathema to the plant and bee world. There is little to communicate other than lack and loss. The seasonal interrelations are missing, and the plants and bees dwindle and perish.

Rather than bearing life into the future, humankind has taken it upon themselves to harm and kill, thinking they are alone in the world, thinking life doesn't matter. When humans think themselves alone and kill without regret, they create a world where they are alone, a world bereft, a dying world. Where none survive, Nature will renew, will start again but without humans. Nature will knead them back into the dough and create something new.

PLANT FERTILITY

"Tasting Spiritual Nutrition"

Three seasons of the year, our farm is in full bloom. We start with the earliest blooms of willow, hazelnut, and witch hazel in late winter and carry through to the last hurrah of goldenrod, asters, borage, and sedums — flowers stopped only by the kiss of a heavy frost. All the time in between we have pollen and nectar sources galore.

Our bees visit all the flowers, yet not in the sequence they open. I sometimes wonder why our bees aren't all over some blossoms — ones I know they like — that seem ravishingly perfect for harvest. Yet masses of fragrant rosemary or precious apple blossoms will sometimes be in bloom for days before our bees deign to pay a visit. Why is that?

Then a day later eager parties of enthusiastic honeybees descend on the blue rosemary flowers, and suddenly they can't get enough of them. Apparently bees see nuances in flowers that are beyond my own senses.

This reminds me of my husband, Joseph, whose favorite fruit is a luscious peach. He skillfully picks the ripest peach without squeezing them, as I'd imagine one ought to. Instead he smells them, one after another. His skill at discerning subtleties of scent is finely tuned to ultimate peach perfection. Always, he gets it right. He has ripe peach virtuosity.

Such are the bees, masters of ripe readiness of flowers.

The Overlighting Being

Healthy bees sense wafers in the air near the plants that indicate the presence of peak fertility. Intelligent bees know to visit those plants at the right time. Bees who pollinate the plants engage with the wafers as their unique effects emanate from the planet Venus, marrying heaven with earth. These wafers are not on the wind; they are around and above the plants.

Even though the planet Venus exerts its influence on the plant's fertility, it doesn't all happen at once. Sometimes plants cycle through a few times before their fertility is peaked. Thus some plants come in quicker, and some plants come in slower.

When the wafers alight on or near a plant, the plant, in acknowledgement of the wafer's presence, brings about another process, heightened fertility. The plant emits spore-like ampules, tiny multi-sided molecules, and jets of scent spores slowly explode out of the plant.

Bees with good sensory aptitude readily perceive these signals. The sensing is a 'see- smell' and informs the bees that these blossoms are ready for pollination. Nectar and pollen gathered at peak fertility have more Life Force and provide more spiritual nutrition for bees and for those who eat the honey gathered from those blossoms.

Bees who, as pips, were raised in an appropriate gestational heat are stronger and more perceptive, thus they have the ability to gather the food with the most Life Force and to fertilize plants at the optimal time in the plant's cycle. When the colony's food has a tremendous amount of spiritual Life Force, the nourishment available to the bees is superior and full of energy-giving fuel.

FLIGHT & LIGHT

"Emanating Life Force"

Oh, to be a bee flying over a field of flowers. I know they see the world differently than I do, with a wider array of colors than my human eyes can access. They go out each morning seeking what they love; hoping to find wondrous nectars and pollens that will nourish them and their family. How joyous to have such a relationship with the Earth and sky.

I often think myself a terrible farmer because I find it impossible to pull out all my weeds. Bees love the wild chicory and thistle flowers as much as the vegetables I purposely plant. The bees have taught me to see not just the functional "I can eat this" aspect of gardens but also to witness the Life Force that comes from everything in that garden, even the weeds. Many times I've dug up frisky chickweed, rambunctious vetch and prolific lambs quarters like a good gardener. Instead of tossing them on the compost pile, I've gone off and replanted them somewhere else where they can bloom to their heart's content and make communion with the bees.

Commonly, it's thought that bees seek familiar colors and recognizable flower shapes in the field, but I know they see more and the "more" is every bit as important as the shape and color. They've been teaching me to see the world through their eyes, especially to see the Life Force inherent in each plant.

I read what the bees have said about flight and it keeps bringing me back to the idea that science says bees do not displace enough area with their wings to lift their roly-poly bodies up into the air and fly. Perhaps what they are describing isn't flight at all, but levitation?

This morning, I watched a bee hover in front of an exquisite sunflower. She gracefully landed on a point midway around the ring of tiny spiraled flowers that make up the sunflower's face. In her momentary pause, she was considering the ideal place to begin and, as soon as she found it, she rhythmically collected the nectar from each floret in sequence. In the squash patch, I lifted the leaves looking for treasures ready for picking and found dozens of giant squash flowers filled with exuberant tumbles of golden bees rolling inside, so covered with bright yellow pollen they looked like jewels. The joy of their vigorous connection with the flowers made me laugh out loud.

The Overlighting Being

Principles exist within the spiritual realm that bring forth effects far beyond logic. That doesn't mean these effects don't exist — they just follow principles from another of the many realities that coexist in the natural world.

Such is the case with bees, flight and light. While logic describes bee wings as a surface area that displaces enough air to cause lift, bees fly using a concurrent system that causes elevation, movement through the air and descent.

Bees have a unique relationship with light. Their senses are keen to the many qualities light contains. They see and understand light differently from humans.

Light is laid in layers. The closer to the ground, the more descriptive it is, how it fills the space between life forms. It lies upon the surface of each and reflects an excitatory vibration describing that form's sheath. Beyond color, shape, texture, and reflectivity, light also conveys in another spectrum the life force of the form. Plants, animals, ores, and elements convey their Life Force by engaging with the light through a wave that surrounds them. The plant, for example, exerts an emanation that flows out beyond the plant's surface and interacts with the air around it.

Life forms fulfilling their role embody a joyful assertion of presence and functional productivity, of participation in Life. This assertion emanates into the atmosphere surrounding the life form and shimmers the air around it.

Bees rely on seeing a plant's Life Force emanation to know when the plant is ready to pollinate and gather nectar, to know when a plant is most suited to our co-creative attentions. The vibrating emanation is a visible signal of the plant's success in fulfilling its role and apt progression through its life stages. Bees see this emanation, and are called to gather pollen from these plants. Thus we ensure that the most light-filled plants within our purview are pollinated and carry forth their seed to the next generation.

Life is inherently exuberant.

LAYING THE GRID

"Our Prayer for the Land"

"Whenever there is a birth, death or marriage,
one must go and tell the bees."
~ Old farmer wisdom

My husband and I have a working relationship with our bees. We do our best to let them lead their bee lives as we care for the farm around them. Everywhere we go on the farm we see bees. Their presence surrounds us.

One weekend in May, we had a busier than usual schedule. On Friday and Saturday friends, neighbors and our farm interns helped us gather tractors, backhoes and cords of wood to create a fertile and water-saving planting area for our fruit trees, a method called "hugelkulture." Our crew of volunteers worked and learned alongside us as we dug two ditches each a hundred feet long, four feet wide and three feet deep. We backfilled the ditches with seven cords of logs and brush, then covered them with soil to a height of three feet and planted our young trees into that. Over the next two decades, the wood will rot and create underground fungal growth that will feed the soil life and enhance the soil's capacity to hold its own water, thus keeping the young trees fed and watered. A novel concept with lots of earth moving!

The following day we hosted a farm tour for 35 people. We walked all over the farm talking about the animals we raise, our gardens and orchards, and our approach to working with the land.

On Friday night, the bees conveyed a message that on Monday we needed to take the day off. The bees said all the activity from moving earth and having large groups of people walking around the farm would disturb the safety grid they maintained over our land. They asked us to do nothing on the land all day Monday so they could mend and restore the land. After such a busy weekend, we were keen to accommodate their request and take a rare, but much needed, rest ourselves.

In Our Own Words

Light comes through our wings like prisms. When the sun comes through our wings and pours prismatic colors all around, we experience the transformative power of light.

The paths we move on above the earth create a cartography of flight lines. Each hive is an anchoring point. The lines from each hive go out and come back, out and back. Each hive is a center point of the lines. Each neighborhood is covered by lines that weave over and through the entire area. These flight lines provide a protective web over the earth.

Bees are beings of light, and pollen is light. When we carry pollen back, we have a relationship with light as it goes through

174

our wings. We fly and lay the light path above the earth, like constructing constellations. These paths we make protect the hive.

Our wings also have a relationship with silica. The light coming through our wings is a recreation of a crystalline silica pattern in the earth and in the atmosphere. This brings the silica into the air. Our flights create a garland around the hive, laying silica on the surface of the earth. The activity of the light shining through our wings activates the earth's silica forces, which draws the plants upward.

We jubilantly fly around the hive and take great delight coming back to the hive with our gift. Inside the hive, we are storing the light.

Every time we fly, purpose is laid upon the air. Our journeys are not merely ways to get from one place to another. Our paths in the ether enliven the air, making communications between the earth and the heavens more fluent. Our flight paths exist within the air far beyond the time we fly them. These flight paths are like the bars upon which songs are sung. They are the underlying structure of these earth-heaven songs.

Our flight paths exist much like telegraph wires. The elementals, the planetary influences, the guiding matrix, all have access, and communication flows. It isn't just information because that can be shared many ways. It is that our paths create a convocation of spiritually adept runways upon which knowledge can be shared. Our paths are the 'greased rails' and as such are already blessed avenues for the intermingling of knowledge. The paths, too, are protected as vectors. The more they are used, the more powerful they become. As bees lay new paths and revisit old ones, they connect the places where plants thrive. Visits from bees nourish the spiritual qualities present in the plants, exchanging communications between spirit beings who live within and around the plants.

When we build our protective grid over the land, we also incorporate the heart space energy of those who live upon that land. These protective grids overlap and entwine with other grids, energetically connecting and reinforcing the prayer for the land.

We acknowledge the presence of humans on the land and each, too, is woven into the fabric as an anchor point. A human with a force of will, oriented toward bringing out the goodness of the land and all who dwell there, is an adjunctive support to the work of the bees. A person who listens to the land, who observes and considers forward motion, who provides the needed and requested materials and labor for the development of the land, is known as reliable and woven into the grid. In such a way we recognize and incorporate life-enhancing and life-enlivening 'poles of being' that come from industrious and vivacious adults, children and central animals who contribute to the land's development and progression. These poles of being anchor and stabilize the grid. Thus it is important when any being in the grid leaves or a new being arrives that one 'goes and tells the bees.'

While we do, on our own, notice and accommodate changes, telling the bees provides us with needed information to make timely adjustments in the grid. It respects our work as protectors of the land to communicate to us any major changes on the land itself as sometimes Earth changes may alter source points of Earth energies that we then undertake to repair and strengthen. Telling us of these changes brings us into a deeper and more communicative partnership. This act both encourages and tempers the human will so our wills align with the good of the land, our shared home.

FIELD CAKE

"Sacred Nourishment"

One of my favorite things to do is watch the bees bring in pollen. All day long, bees land on the front entrance, legs laden with firm balls of flower pollen. The hairs on the bee's body have a bit of static electricity, and when bees gather the flower's nectar little grains of pollen get stuck on the bee's body. After getting a good dusting the bee neatens herself up by sweeping her front legs over her head and upper body, pushing the pollen to her middle legs which continue sweeping until it's all gathered neatly on her back legs. Her hind legs have stiff spike-like hairs into which she presses the ball of pollen. If the pollen isn't sticky enough to make a clump, she'll add a dab of nectar to hold it together. When she has gathered enough she flies on home.

That's where I find her, landing on the front board with a heavy load. The pollen color is determined by what flower it came from and often has no relationship to the flower's color. I see shades of yellow from maple, apple, cherry, peach, willow, mustard, clover, dandelion, blueberry, cucumber, melon, sunflower, pumpkin, and goldenrod. Gray pollen comes from blue borage, raspberry and blackberry flowers. Pear and marigold pollens are orange, malva is bright purple. Fireweed has a fuschia pink flower, but the pollen is a distinctive royal blue. Phacelia flower pollen is dark blue. One area of our garden has giant red poppies who give the unusual but easily identified black pollen.

The pollen is used as pip food. It is about one-fourth protein with the rest being a mix of vitamins and minerals, fat, starch, and a little nectar to keep it bound. It also contains amino acids, lipids, and beneficial bacteria. The young nurse bees also eat some of the pollen which helps their wax glands to develop, preparing them for their next job as comb-builders.

If you are a beekeeper and want to make sure your bees have plenty of pollen, you may want to plant heavy pollen producers. Borage blooms from early summer to frost. Goldenrod is a strong fall plant at a time when other bloom may be scarce. Echium bushes put out dense clusters of long-blooming flowers. Lemon balm is very easy to grow and has a long bloom. Exquisitely spiraled purple phacelia flowers are prolific for both pollen and nectar. The Melissa Garden website (www.themelissagarden.com) and Xerces website (www.xerces.org) have good lists of bee foraging plants.

Pollen must be processed before it can be fed to the pips because pollen has a dense cell wall that is not easily digested by the baby bees. The first step is to ferment it. Bees do this by adding a bit of glandular secretions to the pollen as they pack it into the cells, sealing it off with a dab of honey. Microorganisms kick off the fermentation process and, after a few weeks, the pollen becomes "bee bread." Significantly different from raw pollen, the fermented pollen has many more vitamins and a lower pH. Studies have demonstrated that bees who were fed bee bread lived much longer than bees fed regular pollen, giving credence to the idea that the microflora of the hive is more important than we imagined.

A wild-bred Queen — mated with a dozen or more drones as feral bees do — brings plenty of genetic diversity into the hive. In such diverse colonies each different-daddy family of bees will have skills they are particularly good at doing. One line may be great at gathering volumes of pollen. Another may know how to reduce mite populations. Another genetic line may hold behaviors that show they understand how to work well in damp weather or high heat. These qualities may not present themselves until the colony finds itself in a challenging situation. If the Queen has mated with a wide variety of drones from different families, the colony has a better chance of having the problem-solving qualities on hand when needed.

Genetic diversity can greatly have an impact on biotic diversity, as well. Internally, some bee families within this colony may carry a natural capacity for a strong microbiome, the collective family of microorganisms present in the bees. Take this just a step further, and it is easy to see how this biodiversity could provide the colony with nutritional or protective advantages that originated with one small group of bees who then carry their beneficial bacteria into the colony's larger community.

A recent study found that colonies with more genetically diverse populations — feral bees — have 40 percent more active bacteria species in their guts than colonies from a single genetic line. Bees bred in large bee breeding operations are generally from single or narrow genetic lines and would be less likely to have such diverse gut bacteria. Buying bees from big bee breeders is how most beekeepers acquire bees, so it follows that these bees might not be as robustly healthy as many feral colonies are. Genetic biodiversity gives feral, swarming, wild-mated bees a better chance at surviving well.

The study, titled "Characterization of the active microbiotas associated with honey bees reveals healthier and broader communities when colonies are genetically diverse" contained this nugget:

"Because of the way that bee bread is inoculated, matured, and distributed, its microbial community acts as an extended gut for the colony, and the benefits of its activity are shared amongst all colony members."

Years ago I met Laurie Herboldsheimer, author of *The Complete Idiot's Guide to Beekeeping*, at the Organic Beekeepers Treatment-Free Conference. I enjoy her work — she's good at seeing the big picture through small details. She described how microorganisms are responsible for fermenting the pollen and are then fed to the pips to make them healthy. When a beekeeper puts antibiotics into a hive to kill pathogens, it may have the unintended effect of also killing off some very important bacteria that make bee bread so nutritious for young bees. Who knows what deficits would come of that? I was tickled to hear her say this because the bees themselves had just begun explaining this idea to me and hearing it from a more scientific perspective deepened my understanding of the significant role of microorganisms in the bee gut.

The hive is full of bacteria, yeasts, enzymes, and more. The hive environment is clean, and yet it teems with life. A healthy hive has achieved a marvelous balance of life forms that coexist and, together, build health. Give them nutritious forage, let them direct their home security with minimal interference, pray for favorable weather patterns, and bees are likely to do fine.

In Our Own Words

Bee bread we call field cake. Field cake is made from pollen mixed with digestive enzymes that live inside the house bees. Eating the enriched field cake calibrates the pip's digestive system to match that of the hive. Pollen made from a familial bee is far superior to manmade pollen cakes. It is not just fuel; within the cake are families of helpful bacteria. Eating this brings the pips into synchrony with the other sisters and brothers.

These bacteria and yeasts are part of the generative family line, like the DNA of the hive. The DNA replicate in all successive bees, promoting family. Field cake is the medium for the hive's internal flora and is a way for the beneficial bacteria and yeasts to continue regenerating their Life Forces through bees, symbiotically carrying all of them forward in time. Life begets more Life.

Because bees are place sensitive, the pollen they eat tells them of this place. There is a certain joy that comes in a bee when it has eaten some of the pollen as a pip and then goes out and finds that flower's pollen as an adult. That feeling helps them KNOW that this is good for the hive.

Field cake is a layered sentient blend of the light, scents and tastes of the field — food for the body as well as spiritual nutrition and nourishment. The pollens are mixed because that expands our palate and encourages exploration in mature bees. Field cake tells us, when we go out to harvest, to find foods that taste like this.

The preparation of field cake preserves the internal organisms that help us to absorb nutrients, guide immune system responses and maintain good health. Field cake introduces the beneficial microbial and bacterial community to the baby bee, connecting the little bee to all bees who have gone before.

The virtuous internal community has many layers. Each family of bacteria has a different role within the bee's body. Some bacteria break down the story of the cake so it is accessible to the bee's system, sorting and explaining the landscape and conveying a generational explanation of how bees historically relate to the spirit and substance of the plants.

When human medicine is applied to hives, it removes bacteria. This causes us to lose portions of the plant's relationship to our bodies, and we cannot absorb certain minerals. The bee suffers, though it may survive from this omission. Rather than protecting bees, the medicine causes a loss. True medicine would enhance functions, bringing about a deeper harmony within the system.

This is the purpose of the field cake, to strengthen and nourish all aspects of nutrition and build knowledge of symbiotic familial relationships. Human medicine is often medicine of subtraction whereas Nature's medicine works by addition, seeking to build strength and harmony within and between sentient awareness. Excellent field cake stimulates many positive responses and creates a splendid health-filled, expansively knowledgeable bee capable of continually evolving to its fullest expression.

When treated by subtractive medicine, some portions of the microbial community die off. Specific microbes and bacterial communities interact with their partners to create a beneficial interrelated wholeness where land, insects and plants speak with each other. These are building blocks of life. They need to speak with each other in love, directing and encouraging symbiosis, and constantly questioning and acknowledging what enters the bee.

Yes, this is good.
We need more of this. Not too much of that.
No, that has no function here.
Yes, this creates a desirable present and sets an evolutionary state.
Yes, in this moment we become expansive and sing the Song of Increase.

WINTERTIME DREAMTIME

"Remembering Summer"

What does a beekeeper do in winter?

In late fall, I spend quiet time with the bees, sitting at the entrance as they finish foraging the last of the fall flowers. I hope each colony has enough honey put aside to ease through winter and that they have enough bee bodies to keep everyone warm in the cluster. Because of the slowdown in activity, some of the winter maidens stretch beyond their 45 day life expectancy and live through the whole winter season. The last of the drones have departed, and the Queen won't lay more drone eggs until spring. I make sure all my hives are secured with tie-downs so the rare but occasional strong winter winds won't blow them over.

As winter progresses and fewer bees venture outdoors, I have to put my ear up to the hive to hear their presence, the constant low and contented thrum that carries them through the cold to spring. In my part of the country, the Pacific Northwest, it gets cold enough that our bees go in and out of torpor throughout the winter. Not a true hibernation, torpor is a metabolic slowdown that halts just this side of hibernation. If it gets cold enough, the colony stops all movement. Anyone opening the hive at this time would think all the bees had died.

In winter they stay warm by bundling on top of each other like blankets. The outermost bees keep the bees underneath them warm. When the blanket bees get too cold, they burrow back into the cluster to warm up. Once this bee has completed her task of providing warmth to nearby bees, she will ingest a drop of honey from the winter stores to refuel her for what she burned off as a blanket bee. This is why it's best to have plenty, plenty of bees, going in to winter. In a large hive, the blanket rotation is less frequent for each bee and as a result they eat less honey than a smaller over-worked hive would. A large hive can generate heat more quickly with less effort.

At the end of summer I may notice a hive — usually a young first year hive — that doesn't have enough honey to make it through the winter. This sometimes happens with swarms that get a late start. If I've got an extra bar of honeycomb on hand, I may add some comb to the smaller hive. This has a dual purpose. Besides being winter food storage, a densely full honeycomb stores heat remarkably well, providing substantial insulation from the cold. This helps the colony control heat within the cluster with less effort.

With small fall hives, I admit I have done more fiddling than I normally do. Besides supplementing their stores with extra honey, I sometimes ask a small hive if they would consider a merger with a larger hive. Most hives say they want to make a go of it on their own nonetheless, and I let them do that, even with the risk of failure.

A handful of times a small hive has agreed to a merger. Typically, only one Queen survives that merger, though it's not uncommon for a hive to allow the lesser Queen to continue to live in the nether regions of the hive. This goes against common belief but I've seen it happen in my own hives a few times now. It's always a surprise.

In a fall merger, the older bees will eventually die off, but the temporary boost in maidens greatly increases the hive's ability to finish the season more strongly. I've heard it said that doubling the number of bees in a hive brings about three times as much production: $1 + 1 = 3$. Larger hives are more efficient and have plenty of hands on deck to get all the work done before the cold weather settles in.

Every winter new beekeepers wonder, "Can I look at my bees in winter?"

I'm so glad you asked.

You won't see much activity this time of year. On days that have a bit of sun you may see some bees venture out for quick cleansing runs. They fly out fifteen to thirty feet, poop in the air and fly right back inside. Our car is parked due south of two hives and, on winter elimination days, we find a scatter pattern of little orange dots on our windshield. Aside from that, everyone is slumbering in the cluster so I leave them be. Opening the hive will cause a drastic heat loss, too much for the sleepy bees to easily restore, and it disturbs them from their deep rest.

I know many new beekeepers who have had their bees die over winter. When I ask, they often recount a scenario like this: "It was sort of warmish so I opened the hive to have a look. All the bees were dead on the comb so I cleaned out the dead bees and took the remaining honey. I'll try again next year."

Let me take this story apart and tell you what most likely really happened.

"It was sort of warmish..."

Below 65 degrees is sort of coldish to bees. If you're not wearing shorts and a t-shirt, it's a cold day in bee-land. Under 50 degrees and bees no longer have the capacity to move.

"...so I opened the hive to have a look."

Opening the hive releases any little pocket of heat they have. In winter it's really hard for them to create and maintain heat. When they need to make heat, which they do by shivering, they eat more honey, which depletes their saved stores. Over the course of the winter, less activity is better because it conserves their honey. Opening the hive in cold weather breaks the propolis seal and the bees aren't in the right mood to rally and repair that.

"All the bees were dead on the comb..."

They may look dead but if they've taken themselves down to torpor they're just asleep. Torpor is a temporary suspensory state, not full hibernation. Torpor is a metabolism slow-down that lets them go into a stuporous sleep that is hard to rouse from. Sometimes, even after it warms up, it can take the torpid hive three days to come back to full movement and function. If there is a frigid cold spell, torpid bees may look like they froze to death on the comb. When you look inside you can't tell who is dead and who is asleep. The bees are deep in winter meditation, communicating with the sleeping flower spirits, and we don't want to disturb that.

"...so I cleaned out the dead bees and took the remaining honey."

Oh no! At this point you can't fix it. Someone called me a few years ago who did just this. He brought the dead hive into the basement, took the honeycombs out and put the honey into jars for the family. A few hours later he went downstairs and was surprised to find the combs crawling with bees. They'd been in torpor and now that they'd warmed up and were awake, he was stuck. He couldn't put them back in the hive to cluster because he'd taken their honey along with most of the comb. Comb with honey on it acts as insulating walls that help keep the warmth around the cluster. He left nothing behind for the bees. They had no home to go back into.

"...I'll try again next year."

If you do, please don't open the hive when the bees are at their most fragile. I get calls like this all the way into spring-time. Best to leave them without disturbance and let them wake up on their own schedule. Give them every good chance to make it through spring.

Sometimes new beekeepers get nervous when they see a clump of dead bees on the ground outside the hive. That's actually a GOOD sign. It means the active house bees inside are exhibiting good hygiene and keeping the hive clean. The number of bees populating a winter hive is a constantly changing number. Older bees die off every week. That is normal.

Every week, I look at the hives on my deck and can count how many dead bees get carried outside the entrance. From there a maiden will pick up the dead body, fly it a few feet or further so it doesn't attract interest from bee-eaters. Then she will drop it and return to the hive. Because this colony is on the wooden deck rather than in the grass, I can easily see the body count of the colony's attrition.

At first, the number of dead bees was alarming to me, but now I know that a hundred dead bees outside the hive on a warm day is fairly normal. If a hive goes into winter with thirty-thousand bees and comes out the other end with twelve-thousand bees, the hive did okay. Even if eighteen-thousand bees died over the winter, the hive is still viable. No matter how much you want to look, control the urge! Renowned beekeeper Michael Bush often says on this topic, "Good news is worth waiting for. Bad news will keep."

In Our Own Words

Winter is the time of the cluster, the dreamtime. The stores are in place, the Queen's laying has quieted and we draw together in contentment. The hive is sealed, suspended in a dreamtime of hive images held by the Unity. Like the swarm, it is time when we dream of Unity, holy days when we say, 'I embrace and am embraced by the hive.' Honey is passed and shared and the memory of the sun's light is in our awareness.

We visit again in our vision the place where we conceptualize the world, where we see a bee visiting a flower, collecting nectar into her. She takes the nectar inside where she mingles it with her own life juices. The nectar she collects contains individual information about that flower and the collective information from that flower's family — its history, intention for the future, and the knowledge of the land from which it comes.

She takes this nectar inside her and joins it with her own single history, the memory and knowledge of this flight, as well as the history of her clan, which is contained in her enzymatic measure of her clan and her individual helix. The little drop of nectar is a map of that flower and this bee's present being which includes a sense map of the past and a directive for the future.

During the winter, we revisit the flowers through the taste and scents of the honeys. Each flower group has a signature we easily know. Though the flowers have died back and are now out of season, their flower essence continues within the hive and within us.

THE SONG OF INCREASE

The honeys are opened in a certain sequence. Denser honeys are better for intense cold spells and lighter honeys are for warmer weather. The nectars are collected and stored in a sequence so they can be eaten at the appropriate times.

Spring honeys fuel our building time when we are most in the Song of Increase. Honey gathered in late summer and fall are best for winter when we slowdown our activity, when we enter the dreamtime of cohesion.

Increase means expansion and creation. Cohesion means connection and community. Likewise these honeys have, for humans, medicines within their taste. Spring honeys fuel industry and activity that expands out into the world. Fall honeys draw us together in Unity and appreciation of community.

In winter dreamtime we unite and communicate with the nascent beings who dream the next cycle's crops into life. When the hive is satiated, content and in the torpor of winter's rest, we revisit the forage lines we laid in place during the harvest. These lines still exist in our collective memory and ingesting these honeys replays for us the nectar paths. The winter bees may not have been privy to the nectar collection of each flower family, yet the knowledge is passed within the collective, like gathering around to read a map and sing together.

Moreover, the presence of each flower group's spiritual beings are acknowledged at this time. The flower spirits are in a torpor of their own in winter. The seeds are in a waiting.

The hive, however, is alive with the presence of these spirits. Dreamtime is a celebration of connection and appreciation, a time of deep spiritual union when we are intensely aware of the flower spirits. In this time the overbeings of the flowers are held in a cupped hand of gratitude, as we send our appreciation, enriching and nourishing the flower beings and encouraging a fruit-

ful next season. Even with biennials, the nourishment progresses the plant.

During winter's crystallization we see a multifaceted gathering of forces within the core of the light workers, our earth's helpers. All is brought together in Unity, like the myriad windows in our eyes reflected into the multitude.

Plants with nutrient and mineral requirements that match the qualities of our area thrive in these soils. These plants send forth flowers whose nectar is gathered during pollination. The flowers, by way of their nectar, convey the etheric signature to the bees. The bees are constantly aware, even in winter. Thus we function as memory-keepers, all the year, of the vibration of the flowers

The hive carries and holds the chemical, mineral and nutrient stamp of that flower's family. It is more than this though. This nutrient analysis is also the language of the planet and a treasury of plant knowledge. We interact with the Nature intelligences throughout the year by recognizing and acknowledging the plants and the presence of the plant beings.

This ongoing confirmation is crucial to plant evolution. In our awareness of the plant's makeup, we confirm, impress and approve the plant's signature. Our 'stamp of approval' injects a joyous Life Force into the plants every time we interact with that plant. This brings a trembling delight to the plant beings and creates joy throughout Nature.

THE SONG
OF
INCREASE

V

"The Song of Increase"

The Song of Increase is the most delightful time in the live of the hive, a time when everything in the hive is blossoming with right action. The bees revel in fulfilling their directive to bear increase into the world.

Two events occur each year that are celebratory keystones in the life of a bee colony. One is swarming, the process by which bees split off from one hive to expand their genetic line out into the larger world and create another colony.

The second event happens after the swarm and the old Queen depart the old hive. They leave behind a bevy of beautiful queen eggs, one of whom will mate and ascend into the role as the new Queen. This new Queen will pick up where the old Queen left off, creating new life in her colony for many years to come.

THE SWARM

"The Birth of a New Colony"

One evening I had a feeling one of our hives was full and needed more space. I mentioned to my husband Joseph that in the morning we ought to add another box to the hive and give them more room to expand.

Twice in the prior days, I had seen big groups of bees come out at midday for the new bee orientation flights, short forays the younger bees make in front of and around the hive that prepare them for transitioning to full time foragers. But something about these flights called my attention and seemed different.

In an observation flight, the bees do a lot of mingling and swinging back and forth as they test their wings while hanging in the air. Just that day and the day before, I noticed groups of bees flew out and hung in the air facing the hive until hundreds of them were outside without a lick of back and forth movement. Ten minutes later, they all went back inside.

Early the next morning before the sun warmed the air, it seemed a quiet peaceful time to add a box. This hive was a vertical Warre hive, a hive where new empty boxes are added on the bottom and when ready later in the season full honey boxes are taken off the top. I placed an empty box on the ground next to the hive so I could put it underneath once Joseph lifted the stacked boxes off the bottom board.

Joseph picked up the stack, and I expected to see an empty floor underneath. Instead, surprisingly, the entire floor of the hive was thickly covered with bees all facing toward the door. The gathered bees looked like a cadre of suited executives lined up, each with a briefcase in hand and waiting for a train in controlled anticipation. They were perfectly still when we lifted the hive body up. Not one bee flinched. They all "got the memo" that they weren't to leave until the sun hit the hive at ten o'clock that morning.

We were weeks too late to add the box. The hive had already determined their space was full and they stood at the ready, patiently awaiting a signal that would tell them to begin the swarm. Sure enough, when the late morning sun hit the hive, they departed in an enthusiastic swarm cloud.

Bees are at their most gentle during a swarm. They have no territory to protect and only one immediate mission — to conceal the Queen as she flies in the midst of them. As the reproductive force in the colony, the Queen is the most important bee in the swarm. The chaos of thousands of flying bees is meant to keep anyone from knowing which bee is the Queen.

Many times, I've walked into swarms always amazed at the complexity of their undertaking. Each bee flies in looping circles, keeping a near-miraculous even distance between and around each bee in the ever-expanding sphere. As I've moved inside the swarm, never has a single bee mistakenly flown against me. Each bee knows the exact location of every other bee, tree branch, person, and any other object near the swarm, and accommodates itself around it.

I have noticed that swarms are very good predictors of sunny weather. We grow and bale our own hay on the farm. We need to know when the weather will be dry enough to cut the hay and leave it drying on the ground for a few days before baling. Knowing a spate of warm and sunny days is on their way is a huge help. Rather than listening to weather reports, we pay attention to swarm activity. When my phone rings with a few swarm calls before noon, I know that means there will be a break in the weather and I tell my husband it's a great day to make hay.

The bees know weather and uncannily seem to know when it is safe to venture out. I won't say this is one hundred percent reliable because I do find wet swarms occasionally but that could happen because a swarmed hive didn't find a new home quickly enough and got stuck hanging in a tree so long that the weather changed. Generally, they are good at predicting sunny days. Once in my own bee yard, I saw a hive swarm to a nearby tree and park themselves on the tree limb for an hour. When the sky suddenly clouded up they moved back into the hive and waited inside, dry and safe, until the next clear day.

Each spring as the flowers come out, colonies go through a big growth spurt called "building up." Longer days and warmer weather draw the bees out into sunshine where blooming trees, bushes and field flowers beckon. By nature, bees are industrious. They gather pollen and nectar to feed everyone, build comb to fill with food and new bees, and the Queen lays thousands of eggs to increase the colony's population. The intent is to completely fill the hive and most colonies do that well.

Living in the Unity, every bee in the hive is aware of the status of the colony's health and production at every minute. Knowing the colony is nearing peak capacity and ready to reproduce another entire hive thrills them and activity ramps up even further.

Each spring my hives swarm. They do this when everything in the hive is perfect — plenty of eggs close to hatching, pollen ready to feed the pips in the nursery and as much honey as can fit on the comb. When there is no more room in the hive to place eggs, pollen, or honey, the colony reproduces itself by leaving all the fruits of their labor behind and going off to create a new hive on its own, from scratch.

Swarming is one of Nature's most remarkable methods of reproduction. A swarm departs the hive with two-thirds of the bees and the Queen. These bees will setup housekeeping in another location, essentially moving the old hive's residents somewhere new and creating another living community of bees. They leave behind the younger one-third of the colony to care for the babies as they hatch and to prepare for the new Queen's birth.

The house bees will continue to prepare the empty cells for the Queen to lay eggs into each day. In times of abundance when plenty of flowers are in bloom, the colony may expand its honey area to wherever they find empty cells, including the brood area. When a colony has no more brood cells to fill because they are all full of honey, the hive is called "honey-bound." There simply are not enough empty cells for the Queen to continue laying new brood in and the colony's growth stops.

The bees know the hive is nearly full and they begin preparations for swarming. They make sure the Queen has filled enough queen cells to ensure a new queen will hatch out and replace her after they leave. Even before the colony departs, the scouts start looking for a new home. If those lucky bees have a potential home arranged before departure, that means they will swarm, land on a branch for a few short minutes to make sure the Queen is with them, then fly off to their new home and get started building. Either way, these preparations for swarming are extremely exciting and leave the hive humming with activity.

Healthy bee colonies revel in two peak events—swarming and developing a new Queen—yet both of these are often denied them in conventional beekeeping. When a hive swarms, about 2/3 of the bees will leave to start a new hive elsewhere. Such a big decrease in the workforce means less honey, therefore, less money for beekeepers who sell honey. Another reason for denying the colony the joy of swarming is to "protect the public" who is often misinformed by the media with inflammatory stories that reinforce fear of bees.

In conventional beekeeping, queens are not allowed to fly out and mate with wild and strong local drones. Instead queens are artificially inseminated to keep the bloodlines pure, or they are grafted, a process that creates what we call "emergency queens."

In most conventional hives, queens are purchased from queen-making companies. Nearly always, these companies provide grafted or artificially inseminated "emergency" queens. I learned about emergency queens from Gunther Hauk, a well-respected author and biodynamic beekeeper who has been an advocate for naturally-raised queens. To understand emergency queens, first let's look at how bees create a new queen when they need one in a hurry, as when their old Queen unexpectedly dies.

Upon the Queen's demise, bees will take a 1-3 day old maiden egg and quickly make changes in her birth chamber and diet that will turn the maiden egg into a queen. The egg develops and hatches into a queen, but the hive always knows she is a replacement queen and not a "true queen" who was destined for queen-hood from the start. Generally an emergency queen is quietly replaced in her first three to twelve months with a true queen who was raised to take her place.

Emergency Queens may have vigor and build up quickly at the start, but they are not known for longevity. Conventional beekeepers typically kill their old Queens (called "pinching the Queen") and replace them at the end of their first year because it is common knowledge that their fertility rapidly declines after that. Why would a perfectly good Queen suddenly become less fertile? The key lies in the regenerative effect swarming has on a mature natural Queen.

During swarming a magnificent event occurs — the Queen's fertility is renewed. When the Queen flies with the swarm into the light of the sun, the sunlight replenishes her hormones and insures her reproductive ability for the coming year. In this way, through swarming, the Queen keeps her fertility intact for up to seven years.

Alas, many hives are forced to operate according to a bee-keeper's agenda and sadly, that agenda often prioritizes honey production instead of the evolutionary needs of the bees.

Now, on a happier note, let's hear what the bees have to say about the joyous event of swarming.

In Our Own Words

When we make new Queens, we sing the Song of Increase. Swarming is an expression of gratitude for the colony, a proclamation of work well done. The Queen toils in darkness all the year except for this one brief time when she emerges into the Light.

An ascended Queen stores Light like a holy sacrament within her. She doesn't need a lot, nor often, but she does need to come into the Light once each year to renew her fertility. Her brief annual flight reconnects her with the Sun. The Sun's Light on her body stimulates her reproductive system, a symbolic remembering of her mating flight, and renews the fecundity, the Life Force, within her.

This is not merely a random moment of brightness flashing upon her. The entire mature community participates and is integral to this renewal.

Soon the moment comes when it's time to leave our old home. We who are departing fill our bellies with honey, enough to last through our journey. We make joy, like a bon voyage, a celebration. The hive is filled with anticipation and exhilaration.

Everyone who is leaving moves toward the open door in high excitement. We pour out of the hive like water.

When we leave the old hive, we come out and fly in rings and loops. We color all the spaces with our presence. This is an expression of joyful excitement at the imminent increase we are embarking upon. In the flurry and whirling, we create a veil for our Queen.

And now the Queen emerges into the swarm. Sometimes the Queen has done this before and has a memory of flying and floating in the air surrounded by the hive bees. The Queen glows in the Sun's Light. She flies freely in the mass of bees, the entire hive surrounding and concealing her as she drinks in the Sun's nourishment. In swarming, the Queen mates with the Sun again, a joyful orgasmic culmination and celebration of purpose, duty and destiny. The sounds and movements are foreplay to the swarm's orgasm, each step fully expressing the hive's mission of continuing fertility. The swarm provides safety for her renewal. The Queen opens herself energetically and physically, inviting the coming year's fertility. The Sun's Light reaches into the Queen, initiating a chemical process that unlocks and vitalizes the coming year's gen-

eration of sperm and seed and thus renews the hive. In her beauty she flies among us, just as she dwells within the heart of the hive.

This is a celebration of our increase, and nectar-laden we each are, the sweetness of life within our bellies. We especially like the spring honeys for our journey because they center us on a map of our lands, immersing us in the scent and flavor expression of the plant life we serve as the messengers of the flowers.

Those bees left behind in the old home are younger bees who are still in the roles of the house bees — nursery tenders, comb builders, pollen fermenters, nectar makers, cleaners, and guard bees. We who departed with the swarm are all foragers, mature bees.

As we fly out, each bee has an energetic cushion around her and we are intensely aware of all the bees around us. During a swarm, we have heightened perception. Even though the swarm is moving in every direction, each bee is aware of all the cues going through the swarm. In an instant, we sense that everyone who is coming is with us. In that moment, flying in all directions becomes flying in one direction.

In the landscape a spot is picked to alight, and we fly to that spot and coalesce into the swarm body. Holding onto each other, the central bees holding onto the branch. Layers of bees take hold of the bees they land on. Each and one, we are breathy, cheerful, adventurously elated. When we alight on a tree, we sing 'All is well, we are in the hands of God.' We land and gather with no protection but our number.

Upon alighting on our branch, we embrace. We clasp each other creating an interlinked mesh, hand to foot. Layering as a gilded swarm, abreast of each and ready to begin anew.

SWARM SCOUTS

"Finding Our Home"

I thoroughly enjoy communing with swarms. A swarm looks like so much boisterous disordered chaos but it's far more organized than one would think. To start, all the departing bees consume a drop of honey before leaving so they have enough nourishment to sustain them for a few days. The first task of the swarm, the exit, lasts long enough for the bees to leave the hive. My hives seem to do that in about ten or fifteen minutes, and I've been lucky enough to witness it many times.

There's a telltale sound a swarm makes, and after all these years my ears are turned to it. More than a few times I've been outside and far from the hives when I suddenly heard a voluminous hissy thrum calling to me. Whatever I was doing falls off my to-do list and answering the swarm becomes my higher purpose.

The intention of the swarm at the start is to create chaos and from the outside, that's just what it looks like, bees flying in every direction in an ever-expanding sphere. Finally, when the air is full of bees, the Queen will join them, though you'd be hard pressed to see her in the clouds of thousands, and that's the point. The bees create enough commotion that their precious cargo, the beautiful Queen, stays hidden amongst the many and thus protected from anything that might cause her harm. Once everyone is in the air, they raise the energy even more, doing the bee equivalent of whooping and hollering. The scene is pure exuberant happiness.

Once the Queen is enswarmed and has flown in the sun's light for a while, the swarm's purpose changes. Now the swarm seeks to congregate to find a place to land and gather themselves together. The transition happens so quickly it is startling. One minute thirty-thousand bees fly about in what looks like disorganized bedlam, and then suddenly there is a focus point — a nearby tree branch — and they fly to it and begin landing one atop the other in a ball. As they land, they form themselves into a hanging elliptically shaped cluster, like a football. The first layer of a few hundred bees grips the branch and each successive bee grabs onto another bee's legs until they become one hanging mass of bees. When all the buzzing bees have landed, they quiet into a soothing hum, resting in place, waiting for the scouts to find and communicate where their new home will be. The swarm cluster won't move again until a new home is discovered.

This may take half an hour or, if nothing seems right, a few days. During this time they patiently wait, docile and meditative, in quiet rapture.

If the swarm has made itself known, this is the time a lucky beekeeper collects the swarm and moves them into an empty hive that will become their new home.

Gathering a swarm and inviting them to live in one of my hives is one of the most sense- enhancing gleeful tasks I know. Often I find them on a tree branch, and moving them is easy. I place a box directly underneath the swarm and give the branch a good shake. The majority of bees fall in a clump into the box. A few hundred may rise up in a brief buzzy cloud, but if the Queen is already in the box, all the bees outside the box will find their way inside to be close to her.

Every so often the swarm lands on something that's not as easy to shake as a tree branch and I have to get creative. I have removed bees from a cyclone fence, inside a pipe, under barn wall shingles, in a porch sconce, and inside the bottom compartment of a barbecue grill. A friend once collected a swarm from the back-seat of a derelict Volkswagon beetle!

"How does one do that?" you might ask. If they are on flat surfaces, I used to sweep them up with a soft whisk broom, but early on I realized bees don't like being rushed so I prefer using my favorite bee tool — a long sturdy turkey feather. Because we have a farm we always have plenty of different sized feathers and the bees seem to like feathers just fine. I say, "Here comes the bus. If you want a ride over to the other bees, jump on," and to my delight, they climb aboard.

Once my bees swarmed onto a very leafy wisteria in our front yard. I couldn't figure out how to get the bees off the vines and into the box. I had handled a hundred swarms at that point and knew how calm they could be so I decided to use my hands. I was concerned if I wore gloves I wouldn't be sensitive enough to feel myself squeeze or injure a bee so I went bare handed.

Each time I have placed my hands into the middle of a swarm I am surprised by the heat. The center of a swarm can reach more than 90 degrees! The warmth is all-enveloping.

I instantly felt myself come completely present with them, not a thought in my head but the mystery of bees. I tenderly eased my hands ever so slowly into the swarm. I felt the gentle movement and benevolent breath of the cluster as they sweetly opened a narrow path for my hands to enter their body, a holy and gratifying moment.

Moving a swarm with bare hands isn't something to be done lightly or it likely won't turn out well. Be thoroughly familiar with swarms and capable of maintaining a sustained meditative state before you do this. They are small innocents and require that we care for them with likewise virtue.

Even the best laid of my plans don't always coincide with what the bees have in mind. In my bee yard last week I collected a good-sized, healthy swarm. I got the bees all nicely housed in a top bar hive, and stepped back to have a look. I know they prefer their new home be a good distance apart from their old home, but they were just settling in. I decided to leave them there until their scouts returned. Then I could move all the bees together to a new location further away. Alas, about 20 minutes later the swarm suddenly mobilized a quick departure and abruptly left.

The scouts found a place that was more to their liking. The speed of their leaving tells me they probably had decided upon their new place even before they swarmed. My swarm collection was merely an inconvenient delay. Sometimes they do that.

Off the bees went in a buzzy, 70-foot-high cloud. My farm interns and I followed the swarm, but lost sight of them when they went through a forest of tall pines, flying like the wind. Though running full speed, we simply couldn't keep up.

My experience is that scout bees, upon returning to the swarm site, can miraculously follow the scent trail left behind after a colony departs. Late in the day, I have seen scouts land where their swarm had rested earlier, take a few steps around the site, and then rise into the air and follow a scent trail to catch back up with the colony. If the day has been calm, this often happens and the whole hive is reunited.

THE SONG OF INCREASE

On this day the weather had been particularly windy and the scent was too diffused. At dusk I found a few hundred scouts clustered inside the hive I'd earlier placed the swarm in. Queen-less and far too small to be a viable hive, I considered taking a spare queen cell from another hive and giving it to them, but there really were too few to make a go of it. I put a few bars of honey-comb in with them and the bees happily stepped onto the familiar surface to wait for their colony's hopeful return.

A Queen-less hive has a certain sadness to it. Over the next few days, the scout bees, though foraging and doing bee-like things, appeared dejected and energetically resigned to fail. I wondered what to do with this forlorn little group. I thought about another hive in the bee yard that could use a few more helpers and decided to add the scouts to it.

I had given the little band of scouts a bar with empty comb on it and for the past few days they had been foraging and filling the comb with nectar, trying to keep up their bee behavior. Nor-mally, I would do a merge of two hives by placing a few sheets of newspaper between the hive boxes to get the two groups of bees used to each other and letting them merge on their own terms. But these bees looked so downhearted I didn't imagine they would be a threat to another hive.

So I made a small opening at the top of the other hive and, a feather-full at a time, I ferried the bees over to the entrance of their new home. This little band of bees had not a moment's hesitation to enter the new hive. Nobody in the older hive even questioned their arrival.

I spent a half hour collecting the remaining bees with a clear shot glass and a small index card, my best single-bee-catch-ing method, and releasing each one at the top opening. As I put the feather or the glass next to the opening, each bee dashed through the opening like it was their long-lost home.

This isn't a big deal, but moments like this are the ones I find so rewarding. A few hundred bees will survive, and I had something to do with it. There are so many times when I wonder if what I'm doing is the right thing and here, watching the lost bees sprint inside, I knew it was.

In Our Own Words

Once we have landed, our scouts begin seeking a new home. If some scouts have already found places in the area, they direct the other scouts with their dance and the other scouts check it out and come back. Even though a scout bee goes out and finds a potential new home and reports back to the swarm with its location, that bee has no sense of individuality with that task.

Before the scout bees leave the swarm body, there is an energetic membrane around the swarm. When they fly off to scout, they don't disengage from that membrane, they extend it out to the locations they are scouting. The swarm experiences the location directly on the scouting trips. The membrane is like a golden bubble.

The scouts are our senses as they search for our home. They enter each possible home and communicate back information of each place's suitability. When a scout enters a potential hive home, she stands within the cavern and emanates a projection of this place filled with comb and in its fullest expression. She is not 'looking' at empty space; she is seeing the place as a full working hive. She notes especially the movement of air within, how readily this can be modified to protect the broodnest. Though size is significant, the air within is even more so as the brood is our utmost concern. So also we want a hidden and defensible entrance.

The sound of the vibration inside is important to us, the

resonance, because communication is so vital to us. The warmth of the space is important and enough size to expand the colony as it grows.

We also prefer a fall-away so that anything that should not be in the hive upon us can fall away and keep us clean and healthy. When we live in the tree, what we groom off falls down into dried comb and litter where it can't come back up. The fall-away is part of our medicine and a key to how we maintain the health of the hive.

As each scout returns, she dances the information and the other scouts take off to have a look. The visit is, for each, a time to envision the working hive and news of the suitability moves through the swarm. We all have an accumulating image-sense of these possible homes in the projection details as they are inspected and communicated.

The dance gives detailed direction to where the potential home site is, but the projection has already been delivered. Within the swarm, each of us perceives from the perspective of the 'wholeness of being the hive,' our likelihood of thriving within this new home. We see ourselves already living there and the ease and comfort we will share within that place.

As news of these locations passes through the swarm, we find one location more desirable. The communication of each location has been shared, so we are all part of the selection. There is no separation from the knowledge, as one bee entering that place is by nature the senses of all the rest of us. Her emanation within the space is carried to all of us. Thus there is no need for the swarm to visit each possible location. The scout, and other scouts who accompany with follow-up visits, express in their emanation the suitability of each location. The emanation expressed within that location is the first layer of how we will create our home within this space.

When a location is less suitable, we see that, too. When follow-up visits continue to express the shortcomings of a location, we lose interest and that location recedes in our consciousness.

When enough scout bees extend the membrane to a specific location with a sense of approval, the knowledge of our new home emerges in our awareness and we depart henceforth straight to the hive-to-be. In the air of this flight, we and our Queen lay a scent-trail for scouts who return later to follow.

Once inside our new location, each bee adapts to a new role and we begin our work. As mature bees, the swarm bees have outgrown the ability to make wax like younger bees do, yet because the new hive needs wax makers we are capable of turning back time in our development and once again producing wax. When our hive needs a function, we come up with a solution.

THE QUEEN'S MARRIAGE

"Reuniting with the Sun"

A virgin queen is treated just like any other bee and gets no special treatment from anyone in the hive until she has mated. If she asks, feeder bees will share food with her like they do with the rest of the colony. That first week after she has hatched is spent in waiting. Her body needs time to mature before she is ready to go on her marriage flight. For this reason I write about unmated queens with a small 'q' and I capitalize 'Queen' after she has mated and established herself as the hive's reproductive force. The mated and ascended Queen is the true mother of the colony. Let's talk about how that happens.

A week before a swarm leaves to make a new hive, the departing Queen deposits eggs into vertical queen cells. All these eggs will hatch but only one of these will become the colony's new Queen.

A week after the swarm departs, the group of 12-15 virgin queens hatch within a few days of each other. Why so many? Nature encourages redundancy so there is less chance of failure. Having a dozen backup queens ready in case the first one (or several) doesn't survive is wise.

The young queens emerge from their cells in the darkness of the nursery. They crawl along the walls exploring the comb, touching the other bees as they work their tasks. As they wander the halls, feeder bees give the queens nourishment. A week later, the young queens are strong enough for their marital flight so they find their way to the hive entrance, to the light. At last they stand on the front doorstep, basking in the warmth of the sun.

When a virgin queen is ready to mate, she leaves the hive with a small contingent of maidens who are familiar with local foraging areas and can help her find her way back home after mating. The young queen searches the sky for the area where the drones gather each warm day, waiting for virgin queens to arrive. These drone congregation areas bring together drones from different hives, thus offering mating queens an expansive range of genetic diversity. Drones from as far as two or three miles away gather in these common regions, which the bees call a "scarp," all waiting for the virgin queens. On sunny days, the scarp is fully populated with drones from many colonies. The eager drones arrive an hour before the virgin queens appear. The drones fly in long looping circles, their enormous eyes wide to the skies, watching for a virgin queen's arrival, reading the air for the seductive alluring pheromone that announces her readiness to breed.

Once the big-bodied drones see the queen, they chase after her in hot pursuit. Only the strongest, most determined drones will catch and mate with her. The first drone who catches her grabs her with his legs and inserts his phallus into her at which point she contracts her abdominal muscles, drawing the sperm mass into her, and pops the joint between his phallus and his abdomen. The drone falls to earth, his reproductive organ still implanted in her. The left-behind organ pulses with an ultraviolet light readily seen by other drones who hurry to catch and mate with her. One drone after another, a dozen or more, each with his own unique genetic diversity, mates with the queen. As each drone donates his sperm, the new queen gathers an enormous range of potential behaviors and characteristics for her offspring. For the rest of her days, the sperm from this glorious mating frolic keeps her fertile and fruitful. Once her marriage flight is completed, she will never again mate nor race headlong into the sun.

When the queen returns to her hive after this flight, she cleans herself up and then seeks out and kills all the other virgin or mated queens she finds. Once the queens are reduced to one, the remaining Queen is then welcomed as the hive's new reigning monarch and given a full royal court of attendants to serve her every need.

Occasionally this last scenario works a tad differently. If the hive truly is overflowing with thousands of extra bees, the Unity may imagine the colony capable of throwing off a second and maybe even a third swarm to create even more new colonies. In that situation, a contingent of guardian maidens may form a wall around some remaining unhatched queens to prevent the new Queen from killing them all, reserving a few who will soon also become swarm leaders.

A few days later, the new Queen begins her role as mother of the colony. Except during cold winter months, she will lay fifteen hundred and up to two thousand eggs a day. She continues creating new life for five to seven years. Barring accident or illness, she will remain the reigning Queen until she and her grown colony swarm the following year, leaving behind new virgin queens to take her place.

This is only the briefest of explanations about the Queen's mating flight, yet covers most of what is conventionally understood about this process. Yet there is so much more to this story! Let the bees tell you about this epic journey of sunlight, longing, becoming, and the mingling of earth and body consciousnesses.

In Our Own Words

When the virgin queen emerges from her cell, she moves first downward to the Earth. Unmated and newly born, she is nearly invisible to the hive, her role yet empty. She moves within the hive with curiosity but not yet commitment. As virgins, multiple queens may pass through the hive corridors, but, until mated, none will ascend as Queen. Unmated virgin queens are singularities within the hive, not yet manifest, nebulae in the hive's periphery. The untouched and virginal queen is a promise as yet unsealed.

The young queen wanders the halls, free of the weight of her future duties. She will wander for a few days, gaining the strength needed for her marriage flight.

As the virgins walk the hallways waiting for the right weather, they may emit a sound, a quick burst of energy that speaks to the Sun. It is a call to the Sun, a promise that she is coming. The sharp sound made by the virgin queens opens the clouds. This vibration of focused diffusion brings the mist in the air, if heavy, to rain, or if spare, opens the light. The noise the virgin queens make is called a harken, a solar harken, an announcement.

This spike of energy aligns molecules to open the air, causing clouds to burn off. The virgin queens call to the sun, over and over, sending the sharp sound out to the gray skies. The vibration goes out from the hive and cuts a brief horizontal slice in the clouds. This pushes the diffused moisture-laden clouds or fog into more condensed areas that, once made heavier, may break the weather. The virgin queens call to the Sun, enlivening areas of stagnation in the air, bringing movement to the atmosphere. This is a relatively rare sound, a call to the water sylphs to help free them from their dream time and open the door that brings them into the world.

When the weather is right, she finds her way down to the hive entrance, to the light. At last, she stands on the front door-step, basking in the warmth of the Sun. The virgin queen's flight is a marriage flight, the only time she mates with the drones.

The earth has a light of its own deep within it. Across the land there are energetic openings in the earth's surface called lumens where the earth's light and sunlight joyously communicate with each other. Earth's light interacts with the Sun, singing earth's planetary signature and contributing to the blended symphonic sound of all the planets' chords.

Inside the sparkling cone-shaped lumen, the earth focuses on the Sun's light in acknowledgment of the earth and Sun's gravitational relationship. The natural mating flights of honeybees take place in the lumen, in portals visible to drones and queens.

These light-emitting areas where the Sun speaks with the earth are gravitationally uplifting places of great levity and the drones know this. The drones' wondrous eyes are capable of seeing the lumen glow, another function of how their eyes differ from the maiden bees. Within the lumen, the gnostic drones spin and whirl, taking great delight in the lightness of the air that buoys up their heavy bodies.

Drones are drawn to a specific place within the lumen often a few hundred feet up where a higher focus of intention occurs. Humans named these locations drone congregation areas but to bees, the drone site is called a scarp and known to all the colonies in each area. Drones from all the nearby hives spend much of their afternoons drifting in the scarps.

When the Sun moves to midday, the drones emerge from their hives and hasten to the scarp. The drones fly an embosoming blanket, drawing circles and lemniscates over and over, laying the sheet of the virgin bower. They weave a bed of prayers, a holy sanctuary of tremendous knowledge and healing.

When the virgin queen emerges from her hive, she surveys the landscape looking for the lumen. When she sights it, she spreads her wings and flies directly to it, entering the lumen low in the light cone. Once in the lumen, the lumen's glow turns everything on in her, illuminates her, even changing her color. The light opens and turns on her knowledge of her role. The drones in their Creation Song sing of this moment to the pips.

In her hive birth, the queen was born into her body. The lumen birth bears her now into her life purpose. Upon entering the light, the queen is quickened. Blessed by the light as in a christening, she is made holy.

At the base of the lumen she aligns herself over the opening and focuses her intent on the upward vertical ascent. The beacon of light that emanates outward from these earth energy points is charged by her stimulatory energy as she flies up and into the lumen.

Though humans may think the purpose of the young queen's marital flight is only to mate, the new queen flies with a more developed intention. Her maiden flight has deeper purposes that raise her into the sky.

She was born with a fundamental imperative to deliver her hive's message to the Sun. This message describes the situation into which she has incarnated and the conditions about her as she rises to the mating. In delivering this message, she unlocks and begins her metier as Mother of the Hive. She shares this commu-

nication about her and her hive's physical and spiritual genealogy as she opens herself to the Sun.

Her next message is to the heavens: each virgin queen carries a distinct sound in her, an audible vibration of joyous expectation. When the queen pierces the earth cover during her mating flight, she shoots a bolt of knowledge — all that hive is aware of — in a message from earth, launching it outward to the planets, conveying the progress being made on earth.

Later, when the drones sing this moment to the babies, the bees hear this part of their history in the birth song. When the drones sing the birth song, they sing about the lumen, how the queen is blessed and made holy as she ascends in the lumen's Earth-light, and the knowledge of her purpose comes into her.

The lumen causes her pheromone to bloom, expanding the scent of her holy purpose. Beginning below the blanket of drones, she rises at great speed till she pierces their circling field. She flies straight up toward the Sun through massed layers of drones, spreading her scent. When the scent enters a drone, he becomes singularly focused on catching and mating with the young queen.

She flies upward toward the Sun as the knowledge unseals and opens in her. Information pours in. She glows and becomes stronger. The drones, with their wonderful eyes, see the light filling her. The drones see things maiden bees are not privy to and this is one, witnessing the light filling the young queen.

As the drone launches himself upward, the gravitational force pushes on his abdomen, forcing his phallus, till now unbidden, down and out from the base of his abdomen. Ready for mating, the fastest drone reaches the queen, joins her, delivers his seed in the tumult of creation and falls backward to earth, dying before he reaches the ground. The next drone reaches her, removes the first drone's remaining part and joins her, each drone successively entering her and delivering his seed.

This union of each is a spark, a cumulative bright light that bursts into the atmosphere. Each consecutive union renews the message to the spiritual realm. The sky glows in the lumen, the holy point where heaven and earth merge in creation.

The queen's flight and the drone's mating build the strength of this outward beam. The queen exerts her energy out toward the Sun, and if she continued onward, she would exhaust herself in flight. The drone reaches and embraces her. He fills her with his seed. She flies on toward the Sun, becoming more whole, more holy, until at last the weight of her knowledge and the compass of her seed turns her earthward, toward her hive and her new life as Queen.

The scent of the mated Queen tells the hive she has, at last, arrived. Upon entering the hive, the last drone's appendage is removed. She sets herself in order and dispatches any remaining unhatched maiden queens. If necessary, she challenges and defeats any other queens who had a successful mating day. Once the details of her preparations are handled, she is ready for the hive to acknowledge her ascension, which they do. The hive immediately and totally aligns itself to her role and her purposeful presence. A calm enters the colony, and peacefulness fills the land.

These mating sites, the scarps, are earth acupuncture points, each a fountain of renewal for the earth, sending knowledge out to the heavens and coursing an acknowledging energy deep into the Earth. This piercing energy is a union of heaven and Earth. It is of great import that these Earth acupuncture points be stimulated by the natural union of the bees each year at their right time.

The lumens are tremendously holy and often near shrines, as they are themselves holy entry points. People who move through these places feel uplifted in spirit and grounded in purpose.

DRUMMING
THE BEES

I originally heard about drumming the bees from a fellow biodynamic beekeeper, Gunther Hauk, author of *Toward Saving the Honeybee*. When he was at our farm teaching a class, he briefly mentioned that it is possible to use a drum to call the bees into the hive. I searched "drumming bees" on the Internet but most of what I found was about drumming on the hive to get bees OUT of a hive, called "tanging," which I did not want to do.

Without ever having seen drumming done, I decided to try it. A swarm from our farm landed forty feet up a cedar tree on an outside branch, too far from the trunk to lean a ladder, and I didn't have a pole-with-a-bucket long enough to reach them. This was in my own bee yard so I had plenty of time to think. With nothing to lose, I simply went over to the empty hive I'd set up eighty feet away and started drumming on the side of the wooden hive.

Drumming bees is simple. Stand next to the empty hive and use one of the wooden bars to hit the side of the hive in a steady beat. I decided to drum in a four-part rhythm, hard-soft-soft- soft, BAP-bap-bap-bap, like a child's tom-tom rhythm.

Drumming can be inductive for me but not at first. I kept saying to myself, "This is silly. The noise will drive them away. How could this possibly work? I'm lousy at keeping the beat." After four minutes I was bored. By six minutes I was really bored. But I continued, and eventually I fell into the rhythm.

Fifteen minutes passed with plenty of time for me to wonder why drumming might work. I couldn't come up with any levelheaded reason bees would come toward the drumming sound, but I continued on. I mulled over the realization that I was not metrically competent enough to keep even a simple beat. I let the thought go and continued BAP-bap-bap-bapping.

Then in one startling moment, the swarm became a dense bee cloud and lifted up out of the tree and began flying straight toward me! I had called them out of the tree and, remarkably, they were flying down and toward me. Fifteen feet above the ground and twenty feet from me, they suddenly spun around and turned back. I'd guess the Queen wasn't with them so they all went back to the tree. But whoo-hee, I was excited! I'd drummed and the bees noticed!

Well, golly! How did that happen? I wondered what the significance of the drumming might be. Why would that be important to bees?

After I calmed down, I asked what bees look for in a new home. They said they seek, *"Resonance. Our communication within the hive is important. We need good sound and vibration inside."*

Wild bees prefer to live in a hollow tree trunk. A scout would need to visit every tree to see if there is an opening to a hollow inside, otherwise how would bees know a tree is available? I kept thinking of their answer — resonance — wondering how Nature would convey that information to a colony.

If a branch on the tree blows in the wind and bangs against the trunk or if a woodpecker rat-a-tat-tats on the tree looking for insects, the tree would readily announce its telltale hollowness and telegraph to the bees, "There is an empty chamber in this tree you might want to come look at."

Later that day I borrowed a telescoping pole from my neighbor and managed to get the swarm down, but the idea that this drumming thing might work latched onto me. Later in the week when I brought home the next swarm, I gave drumming another try.

Bees can easily get tangled in tall grass so I laid down a white cotton tablecloth on the grass. Using a wooden shingle, I made a ramp from the tablecloth up to the hive entrance. Then I upended the box, dumping the bees onto the tablecloth and I commenced tapping on the hive. The bees on the tablecloth milled about in every direction. I drummed the familiar BAP-bap-bap-bap rhythm. After a minute or two — totally surprising me once again — all the bees turned their heads toward the entrance and started walking up the ramp and inside. It took fifteen minutes for twenty-five thousand bees to climb the ramp and get inside, at which point I picked the full hive up off the ground and moved it to its permanent location.

I must admit, this was WAY more fun than dumping a boxful of bees into the hive like I've done in the past. Because it seemed to work so well, I sometimes incorporate drumming as a way to invite a swarm to choose — on their own — to move into the hive I am offering them.

Recently in my bee yard, a swarm found its way onto the edge of a picnic table. I set an empty hive on top of the table and drummed them up and into the hive. Quite remarkable, it was. Maybe they would have found their way inside without the drumming, but I like to think the rhythmic vibrational sound was the perfect invitation to check out the hive and move in.

THE SONG
OF
INCREASE

VI

THE SONG OF ABUNDANCE

When people learn that I keep bees they always ask if I collect lots of honey. Of course, honey is a superb gift of the hive, but it is most decidedly not the only gift. If you have a hive or two or six, you have in your keeping a fantastical wooden box from which you can sustainably withdraw the makings for food, candles, furniture polish, glue, varnish, medicine, and acupuncture.

A hive of honeybees is that gift that keeps on giving...and giving. Honey provides the makings for magnificently healthy food and drink. Honey also can be used in cosmetics, facials, lotions, even as a sterile wound dressing. Allow honey to ferment, and you have mead, a refreshing and truly mood-enhancing golden wine.

Beeswax is made by the young virgin bees, a detail early church leaders took great delight in. Beeswax candles have lighted many a dark night. I keep a beeswax candle lit when I work in my studio as a way to acknowledge and honor the enlightened labor of the bees.

Add a bit of oil you have a wonderful, healing lip balm. Mixed with other oils, beeswax makes a natural and lustrous wooden furniture preservative. Used on doors, bow strings, wire, windows, zippers, and drawers, beeswax prevents sticking. Blended with pine rosin, it becomes an adhesive. These are a scant few of the dozens of ways beeswax makes life easier and better.

Propolis is medicine for bees and it has a long and respected history as a medicine for humans, too. As with other substances from the hive, propolis has many uses: Stradivarius used it to make a varnish for his fabled violins. For centuries propolis has been used to pack and heal decayed and abscessed teeth.

Then we have the sting itself, an oft-overlooked tool of a protective hive. There is growing interest in the healing art of apitherapy, a therapy in which bee stings are injected into specific points to heal inflammation and illness — like acupuncture, but with a healing and beneficial venom.

Corwin Bell, a beekeeper and teacher in Colorado, shared an ancient use of bee stings during a course he taught at our farm. Historically, Corwin said, the hives themselves were used as an effective form of family protection. In medieval times, people kept skeps — small woven basket hives of bees — in alcoves by their front doors. A small hole was made between the interior of the house and the outside alcove wall, and into this small opening a rod was placed. If intruders showed up at the front door, the householder needed only to poke the rod against the side of the skep, agitating the bees and sending the miscreants running for cover!

And, of course, there are the bees themselves and the profound teachings they have to offer anyone skilled in simple, patient observation of this wooden box filled with wisdom.

Everything the bees make has healing in it, from the comb to the scent of the hive itself. In the following pages, the bees reveal their deep commitment to the healing and evolution of the world, and share ways in which we can assist them, as well as partake of their generous and remarkable medicines.

HONEY

"Kindling the Heart of Fellowship"

As I'm writing this we are in the middle of the honey flow, the time when the most nectar flowers are in bloom. In my area of the Pacific northwest, the honey flow begins when the himalayan blackberry blooms at the tail end of June. Blackberries are a bane to land owners with their thick prickly branches, but their prolific flowers are a boon to bees. That bloom is quickly followed by fields of clover and in my area, sunflowers. In other parts of the country the honey flow begins when major bloom comes forth in alfalfa, locust, citrus, sumac, mesquite, loosestrife, and birds-foot trefoil.

Two days ago, I took honey from a hive. The bees were gentle and sweet, floating up around me as I lifted off the honey box. Not a worried bee among them. I'm ever so careful not to spill a drop because I don't want to incite robbing from other hives who come upon a lick and wonder what other treats might be nearby.

When I do take honey, it is my responsibility not to endanger the hive in any way.

Hive boxes full of honey grace my kitchen table and sit on rimmed baking sheets on the counters. Last night, we started processing the honey. We cut combs off the bars, and my husband pressed the wax with a potato masher to release the honey from the cells, then let it drip through a sieve into the five gallon bucket that has a handy spigot on the bottom for pouring into jars. It's sticky business.

Because I know I'm going to get honey all over, I pull my hair back into a ponytail, put on a short-sleeved shirt, and apply some already dripped honey on my face. I worry less about getting honey on me if I begin by putting it there intentionally; receiving a honey facial is now part of the process. If you haven't experienced this, please do. Honey is a humectant and it brings heavenly moisture into your skin. Man, woman, or child, your skin will thank you for this.

I save honey from my bees. "Hoard" is actually the more appropriate word because even though I harvest it, I don't sell it. I hoard honey in case it is unexpectedly needed to feed a hungry hive. Because I never know when it will be needed, I like to keep two years' worth in my pantry. A few years ago, I acquired a hive in late November from a felled tree. When the tree hit the ground, the area where the bees had stored their honey smashed. All the honey was lost. The bees had no winter food and nowhere to gather any from.

I brought that bereft feral hive home to see if we could save them. My neighbor brought his front end loader and he and Joseph set into place the section of their old hollow tree that survived the fall. I had no idea if they would make it but it was worth trying. We cobbled together their old home the best we could, sawing off jagged parts and blocking up holes. Joseph made a wooden feeder box that matched the interior shape of the top hole and he attached the new feeding area at the top, where their honey would have been stored. Over the winter and spring I gave this hive all the honey I had and I am glad I did. The bees survived and have been a strong hive ever since.

I suggest that if you keep bees, be kind when taking honey. Leave plenty for them, and put aside more in case you have an emergency. Most beekeepers take honey in late summer or early fall, when the season is winding down. I take my cue from old farmer wisdom which says honey is best taken in early summer. At this time of year we know they have made it through the winter and still have plenty of blooming summer weeks to store more. A good idea is to save a few bars with honey still on the comb so you can add them to a hive that needs just a bit more to comfortably make it through the winter. If you keep honey and honeycomb on hand, the issue of whether or not to feed sugar to your bees won't arise. If you run short of your own honey, ask a treatment-free bee-keeper if you can buy honey from those hives. Or see what your local organic store is selling and ask if that honey is treatment-free. If it is, stock up.

I eat honey, and I believe bees ought to eat honey also. Some beekeepers, in an effort to maximize profits, take honey from the bees and feed them back sugar water or (egad!) high fructose corn syrup. I am a stickler about honey, because it is what bees have evolved on. The pH, enzymes, essential oils, vitamins, and minerals are in the correct balance in honey, and that does not happen in any other medium. Bees cannot fully process foods that are foreign to them, like we humans cannot eat grass.

When their digestion is compromised by poor nutrition, bees suffer. A good diet made up of the foods they naturally eat makes a huge difference to bees. These days many beekeepers are taught to take more honey than is good for the hive, figuring they can always feed back sugar to make up the difference. I know this is difficult to hear for people who feed bees sugar, but I stand firm on wanting them to eat only honey. My intent is that everything I do is done with awareness of how our actions affect bees. If I ask the question, "What is best for these bees?" the only answer I come up with is "honey." I can't pretend I don't know what is best for bee health.

On the bright side, when I hear of formerly conventional beekeepers who have shifted to treatment-free methods and no longer feed sugar or high fructose corn syrup, I am delighted. More will come. Let's make clean and kind keeping-of-bees a beacon for more folks who want to be true partners with the bees.

About sugar, the bees have this to say: *Sugar syrup is too high pitched, like treacle. We eat it if we're hungry but it makes our stomachs hurt and makes our singing weak and tinny. Sugar doesn't have the prayer in the food.*

I was deeply moved when I heard them say that sugar doesn't have the prayer in it, realizing that this is a necessary part of what nourishes them. When they process nectar into honey, the entire hive song coalesces into the prayer that blesses their food and brings them true nutrition.

Oh, blessed honey! Rudolf Steiner, a visionary agricultural scientist, said of honey:

> "Beekeeping advances civilization because it makes man strong. Nothing is better for man than to add a little honey, in right measure, to his food. The bees, in a wonderful way, give man what he needs for the work of his soul. When he adds honey to his food he prepares his soul to work properly in his body. Bees ensure that man receives what is right for him. When one sees a hive of bees, one should say to oneself with awe and reverence, 'By way of

the beehive the whole universe flows into man and makes us good, capable people.' "

Raw unprocessed honey is full of vitamins, antioxidants, enzymes, flavonoids, and minerals. Honey that's raw and unheated retains more of its beneficial qualities, which are destroyed by heat. So why would anyone want to heat honey? That's a curious story.

Honey's taste and color are determined by the flower source. Generally spring honeys are quite light colored, like honey made from maple flowers. Summer honeys are more amber, and fall honeys tend to be darker though each of these seasonal assessments have many exceptions. Yet most of the honey you find in stores is the same mid-range amber color.

A good friend who knows I keep bees offered me a few gallons of rich, molasses-tasting buckwheat honey and some crystallized wildflower honey she got from an elderly beekeeping neighbor who'd since passed away. She had never seen brown or crystallized honey and was sure it had gone bad. I explained to her buckwheat honey is always dark brown, that crystallization is a natural process in raw honey, and that honey doesn't ever go bad. Honey is a natural preservative and even when thousands of years old, it continues to be edible. Imagine that! A food from ancient times you can still eat. Like the hive itself, honey has the ability to live forever. How intriguing!

Nonetheless, she gave me the jars because she said her family wouldn't eat crystallized brown honey.

This is what marketing has created. It has removed differences in taste and color from store shelves under the assumption that all honey should look and taste the same. Honeys are heated and filtered to keep them from crystallizing, and all the different varieties are mixed together to produce a muddled mid-range neutral color and flavor.

Raw honey will crystallize over time depending on which flower the nectar came from and, to a smaller extent, how it was stored. Fireweed and goldenrod honeys crystallize in as little as a week. Chestnut blossom honey and borage honey stay liquid for a very long time.

In its most natural raw state, honey is lightly strained to get bits of wax or bee wings out and then it is bottled. In a more unnatural process honey is pasteurized (heated) and ultra-filtered. This extra processing prevents the honey from crystallizing, which means it looks more uniform on store shelves. The downside is that it is less nutritious. If you want to preserve honey's benefits, stick to buying raw honey.

Steiner said that honey was so precious that no adequate price could possibly be placed upon it. Speaking to the heart and soul of honey — what it is and what it can do — Steiner said that the bee is formed by the same force, finely distributed silicic acid, that resides in the Earth and constructs quartz crystals. Honey, having been worked upon by the bee's body, helps bees create wax in a six-sided form. This is an interior image that human beings can use. Steiner believed that all human beings "need these six-sided spaces within themselves. Like bees, humans need nourishment that carries over into our bodies and produces a six-sided effect." I don't fully understand what Steiner meant by "six-sided spaces within," but I know that most people, when viewing a piece of bee-crafted honeycomb, are enchanted with the perfection of the hexagons and how they contribute to the economy of space within the hive.

Manuka honey from the New Zealand melaleuca tree has proven antibacterial qualities. It's especially good for wounds and some research shows it may handle antibiotic-resistant staph bacteria as well. Manuka honey isn't the most tasty honey. It is more of a medicinal honey and is even used in hospitals as a healing poultice on severe burns, bedsores, and skin ulcers.

Honey is a humectant, which means it draws and holds in moisture. When I slathered honey on my face before bottling our honey, I had the added benefit of coming out of that sticky process with lovely soft skin. Using this natural bee gift on my skin is far easier than buying a lotion with a dozen strange chemicals — and probably more effective, too.

As a farmer, I am on the front lines of the clean agriculture revolution. It's important that we be thoughtful about everything we purchase and everything we put in or on our bodies. Beyond good agricultural practices, my husband and I now include putting prayer into the food we raise to help bring it to a state where it provides both physical and spiritual nourishment.

In Our Own Words

Each drop of honey contains the rising helix, which invigorates man through its spiritual forces. Honey filled with spiritual forces kindles the heart of fellowship. Through this bond humans develop respectfulness and love of all beings. The bond of respect for all beings is the core of the growing heart. Through respect, appreciation, and all actions based on an honorable relation, you step into your evolution.

The taste of honey on the tongue is a lightness, a quickening, a deep emanation of the sun's light as all of creation bears witness and answers. One's heart is warmed. We bring this gift and ask that you absorb it into your being with awareness of the generosity with which we offer the fruit of a constantly creating and interrelating world. In this, bee and human become co-creative forces and light workers in the world and in love.

THE STING

"The Fire of Love"

I rarely wear a bee suit to protect me from the bees. My bees are friendly, and I am familiar to them. I pay much attention to how they are when I'm around them, and if they seem concerned or upset, I move slower. Nearly always my bees are sweet and gentle and I can do most anything around them, even pick them up in my bare hands, without anyone getting upset.

Recently, I harvested some honey from a hive in our bee gazebo. After I got the honey down to the house, I realized about a quarter of what I had harvested was still uncapped watery nectar and hadn't yet been dehydrated into thick honey. Nectar cannot be kept at room temperature like honey because it ferments easily and turns itself into the honey wine called mead.

I decided to give the uncapped honey back to the bees. I opened the hive for the second time that day, and put two bars of uncapped honey back on the hive. Normally, I don't open a hive twice in a day and I knew they'd be concerned. I was right, they buzzed me a few times, and I walked a ways away from the gazebo to let them know I respected their boundaries.

I knew the bees were a little testy because I got buzzed, then bumped by a guard bee. Guard bees take on the task of fending off interlopers, which I surely was. The first warning was a loud, distinctively cranky buzz near my face, calling my attention. A moment later she flew straight at me and bumped me, forehead to forehead, her way of saying, "Back off!"

An irritated guard bee has no regard for scale. Even though I'm gigantic compared to her, she still flew right into me and tried to push me back. When a bee bumps you, you have a scant second to take the hint and back up. If you back up ten feet she'll probably leave you alone. If you don't, the next line of defense is a sting. I took the hint and backed up, and no damage was done. She warned me and I did as she asked. A truce.

That night, I looked at all I'd harvested and decided I didn't need to keep as much as I had taken and could easily give two more bars back. The following morning all the hives looked quiet and happy, bees flying in and out their front entrances. My friend Susan offered to help and, together, we opened up the hive and put those two bars of honey back into the hive.

A young colony in the top bar hive next to them had a recent growth spurt, so on a whim I decided to peek inside and see how the combs were coming. The normally calm and even hum from all the hives had the tiniest edge to it, just a quaver higher than normal so I decided to wear a bee veil. I don't generally mind getting a sting now and then but a cranky bee tangled in my hair is decidedly unpleasant for the bee and me. Wearing my veil and quiet as could be, I removed the top of the hive.

Eighty bees came screaming out and I got a half dozen stings on my hands in two seconds! I quickly backed up and put fifteen feet between me and the hive before I turned around. I quickly walked fifty feet away with bees still stinging their hind ends into my jacket and on the screen of my veil. I trotted over to a nearby peach tree, raised my arms into the branches and turned in back-and-forth circles. When bears are chased by bees they find nearby low-hanging tree branches and move around in them. The waving branches confuse the bees who lose sight of the bear as he hightails it out the other side of the branches. That's what I did.

I stepped out the other side of the tree, and listened to the air around me. Two bees were still angrily stinging my sleeve. I brushed the soon-to-be-dead guardians off into the grass and said, "Thank you for your service to the hive." Then all was quiet.

This colony had never ever been feisty. I was completely surprised, wondering aloud what caused the extreme upset, reviewing how I'd handled the bees and finding no error. Surely it was something. What could it have been?

Then Susan astutely pointed out it was the morning after Independence Day. Fireworks are legal in my state and the evening before, fireworks boomed into the wee hours. Many were set off by rural neighbors who live a few hundred feet from my hives. Egad. That must have been it! Joseph and I had been up in the field finishing up animal chores just after dusk and we both noticed how the ground shook from the nearby fireworks. Bees don't like that kind of vibration.

If you have plans to have a look-see in your hives on the day after your bees have been violated by loudness, like mine had been, you may want to rethink that. I am so glad I listened to my intuition and put the veil on!

In case you don't know how to best remove a stinger, here is how. The stinger is ribbed so it stays in the skin after a sting. When the bee punctures your skin with her stinger, the stinger separates from her body. That girl will die because the back end of her abdomen came off with the stinger. The stinger, now free of the bee, continues to pump venom into the site for about thirty seconds.

Most people use a thumb and forefinger like tweezers to pinch the stinger and pull it out. Pinching like that will simply inject all the venom. A better way to do it is to use a single fingernail (your license or library card also work) and scrape the stinger out. That stops the venom pulse and less sting juice gets in.

Back when I was a new beekeeper, I used to be afraid of stings. While I still don't enjoy getting stung, I don't mind so much when I do. I believe the bees know where we could use a bit of sting therapy.

Some folks think they are allergic to bee stings, but most people are not. It is normal to have swelling from a sting — sometimes substantial — and it may take a few days until that area is back to normal. A true allergic reaction involves anaphylaxis that swells the throat up enough to stop breathing, and only a tiny, tiny portion of the population has that response.

Bee venom is a potent mix of anti-inflammatories with anti-bacterial and anti-viral properties. It has been used in the healing arts since the time of Hippocrates, the "father of medicine," who prescribed bee sting therapy as a solution to joint problems and arthritis. Bee venom has the ability to promote healing by stimulating a healthy immune system response throughout the body, and especially at the sting site. The venom wakes up our ability to heal ourselves.

A few years ago in February my husband and I helped an elderly friend prune four hundred yards of grapevines on his farm. The next morning my thumb was so sore I could hardly fold my fingers together. All my fingers and especially my thumb ached.

Later that morning, I was up at the bee house checking on my bees. It was winter so no bees were around, but while I stood there one bee came out for a cleansing flight. At the entrance she readied herself for lift off but then she turned and flew to me instead, landing on my wrist. I was in the midst of another "wonderful bee moment" when she stepped onto the heel of my hand at the base of my thumb, turned her face toward me, and, while looking straight into my eyes, leaned back and stung me.

She certainly surprised me! Once stung there is not much reason to flick the bee off since the stinger has already disconnected. I hadn't been stung in many months so I let the venom pulse into me. Within a few short minutes, my thumb completely stopped aching.

Another time I had seven stitches over a tendon injury and a bee stung me just below the bandage at the base of the seventh stitch. The cut healed astonishingly fast with no residual soreness or disability.

I have had this experience with bees numerous times. Something in my body needs attention, and my typically gentle bees send an emissary on a mission to relieve my discomfort.

Every summer at our county fair, I volunteer at the bee booth. The booth is divided into two rooms. The display room is filled with bee paraphernalia and winning entries on one side of a partition. On the other side is a wire-enclosed ten-foot square area with a live hive of bees inside. Speakers enter the bee room through a screened double-door airlock.

Every half hour, a volunteer gives a talk about bees while standing in the bee cage. Most volunteers wear the bee suit. I want people to know how gentle bees are, so I do my talk without protection. Inevitably someone asks how that is possible and I explain that bees have little desire to harm anyone. They only sting when they worry that they or the hive are in danger. Though the number is higher now, back then I told the audience that I'd only been stung three times in my life, each an accidental sting when a bee got tangled in my hair or clothing and, fearing she was trapped, stung me. No harm meant, just a scared little bee.

That year at the fair I was paired with a beekeeper who has political ideas opposite my own. The bee booth is not, in my opinion, the right place to spout one's political beliefs, but that's what he did. Being of a different political persuasion, I was a teensy bit on edge (understatement). I asked him to skip the political statements and stay on topic but he interspersed his views throughout his bee talk. (With no good intentions I made a small note to self: "Do not tell him his fly is unzipped!")

True bee work requires a kind, loving heart space. I love bees. When I approach bees in this space, it is obvious how life affirming, generous and fulfilling the community of bees is. When it was my turn to go into the bee cage for the demo, I was not in a heart space. Not even close. I stepped into the airlock to the bee cage and WHAM! I got stung right on the top of my head.

I stepped back out of the airlock and untangled the little bee from my hair. I had already pumped some snitty-ness into my system before I got stung, and I was surprised at the adrenaline the sting evoked in me. I shook it off, took a deep breath, walked back in. WHAM! Again, stung on the very tip top of my head. The exact same place as before, my crown chakra, the side of me that points to the heavens although I certainly did not have heavenly thoughts emanating from within.

I stepped out of the cage again, and this time a single bee came outside to have a talk with me. She assertively buzzed me, and in no uncertain terms told me not to set foot in their home until I worked out my "stuff" and bettered my attitude. Okay, I can take a hint. In utter humiliation, I went out and returned in my full bee suit, wearing it the whole time I gave my talks.

Receiving not one but TWO stings in the exact same spot was not lost on me. I admit I had very little loving cosmic consciousness going on when I first reached for the door to go inside the hive room. I was still replaying, "I should have said..."

Luckily my shift was nearly up. As I am not yet an enlightened being, I still had dialogue going around in my head as I drove home, and I was none too pleased about getting stung twice. Once home I changed my clothes and decided it would be a good idea to visit with my own bees and calm everything down.

I walked barefoot through the field toward a hive and WHAM! I stepped on a little bee who stung me in the very center of my foot, on the Bubbling Spring acupuncture point — the very first point that forms in the fetus, the one that helps you ground and connect with the earth, the point that roots energy downward.

I sat down on the ground and scraped the stinger out, apologized to the honeybee for stepping on her (and felt terrible that I'd done that). I told the bee her gift wasn't in vain, that I would sit right there and go over my day and let go of whatever crap I was carrying around that was making me bad bee company.

Three stings in one day doubled my entire life's sting count. Getting stung on the very top and very bottom of my body was none too subtle. I had throbbing focus points showing me precisely where energy runs through and connects me with the heavens and the earth.

I sat there and apologized to everyone I had labeled harshly, had miserly thoughts about, or offended (including my higher self) by being such a knucklehead. And, when I felt I could be a better person, I got up and went on with my day.

I did notice that as a result of having all that bee venom in me, I was intensely aware of ALL of my body, like I was breathing through my skin instead of just my nose. Having a front row seat to an important bee lesson in selflessness caught my attention, and I felt buzzingly happy for quite some time.

JACQUELINE FREEMAN

In Our Own Words

The sting. I inject myself into you; when you sleep, you dream of possibility. Even the discomfort is to awaken you. I kiss to start you up. The turn is the fire of love.

My venom cures disease and purifies the blood by stimulating the cleansing process, but not by removing a substance. No, this cleansing is by transformation. We commingle our matter in a pulsing swelling that rises up like a small hive under your skin. Wild within the small cosmos, it calls your attention. Immerse yourself into this heightened awareness, and feel the helix that is my signature.

I die into you that we both may live.

EVOLUTIONARY
MEDICINE

"Bathed in Sacred Illumination"

Bees are not simply a backyard hobby for me. They are intelligent, respectful, caring beings who are full of commitment and love. I am proud to call them my dear, dear friends.

When I first started speaking with them, I was thrilled to understand the inner workings of the hive, how they interact, what they see as their role in agriculture, and how they envision their larger purpose. With all that, it hadn't occurred to me that they would also expect me to understand advanced concepts of healing and medicine and even quantum physics, which they do.

Some of what they have spoken to me about has set me to researching these topics just so I could comprehend their words and images and continue the conversation. I have sat at my computer asking the internet what a quark is and how the limbic system works. Over time I imagine they will bring many more concepts that will send me back to google again and again. Occasionally in these searches, I come upon information that verifies what the bees have told me, which is always exciting.

Rudolf Steiner, the visionary philosopher-scientist, also saw deeply into the potential of the bee to heal and to assist us in our own evolution. He writes:

> "The consciousness of a beehive, not the individual bees, is of a very high nature. Humankind will attain the wisdom of such consciousness in the next major evolutionary stage when human beings will possess the consciousness necessary to construct things with a material they create within themselves."

Since this project began in 2010 when I first heard the words of the bees, I have of necessity come a long way in expanding my own thinking. To get this bee knowledge out into the people world, I've had to become public about what the bees have said, and acknowledge that this information has come to me from bees. The first few times I spoke of this, self- consciousness made me hesitant and I had to push myself past that self-imposed barrier.

Yet the bees have been clear that they want us to know them in this newer, deeper way. They are always compassionate with my sometimes bumbling efforts to understand them better, and to serve as their voice. In this next conversation, they explain how they can help us become healthier and how they heal disease. They are eager to help us progress into our next evolution and become more caring and connected in a vital way with each other and with our precious Earth.

I began this communication by asking them where bees came from.

In Our Own Words

We are an evolution unto ourselves. We emerged into the Earth sphere as a template of unity, harmony, community. Bees are an evolutionary progression. Our sound expresses a unified community working in harmony.

Scent and sound have the ability to enter the nervous system to provide a progressive adaptation to the environment. The scent and sound of a hive contain compressed information. Scent and sound can rewire our deep inner perception — the matrix of what we operate from — our belief system. This is no small task.

Each hive's great hall is the portal that allows each hive to be present in the consciousness of all hives. Bathed in a sacred illumination, our communal presence kindles the evolutionary intelligence nascent in each being. And thus we begin.

We prepare and build our hive to contain the scent. The air we breathe inside the hive is our medicine as well as our joy. We seal the hive to keep harmful influences outside, to preserve our hygiene and to magnify the forces impregnated in the interior air.

Air is a canvas. Like water it has memory. As we breathe, work and imagine, we imprint the air within our hives with industry, unity, solace, and love. The Unity of the hive is expressed in our sound, which permeates the air. The air within the hive is full of our song, full of the event of us as we fill time forward and back.

We impress the noble scents of nectar, wax, propolis, our Queen, the emotional states of all the bees. Yes, we have emotions but not as separation between us. We feel as one in our individual contributions. The joy of the harvest tasks; the delight in the scent's vapors; we keen in the loss of our Queen; we suffer together in illness or dearth.

A wild hive is sealed and the colony lives in the propolis-

scented hive air, breathing medicines that keep us healthy. Our systems respond to the enumerated quavers by bringing each bee's body to balance and good strength. A hive in good order lives in the healing scents of the medicine we have made for ourselves from plant partners who surround us. This medicine offered by the plant community includes the rising mineral-rich sap of trees, their lifeblood.

Humans will eventually begin to use scent more to heal their bodies and minds. Again, this is medicine by addition rather than subtraction. Subtractive medicine seeks to kill an organism or relationship, but it often has deleterious side effects that further unbalance the organism's health. Medicine by addition restores balance by completing relationships, like keys in locks. In its highest state, medicine by addition further opens the beings to optimal states that create evolutionary expansions that resolve past weaknesses. These advances include the physical states, of course, but they also direct us toward advanced and enhanced intellectual, emotional, perceptual states that often combine and overlap new abilities.

When humans begin participating in medicine by addition, they will strengthen their systems and increase their sensitivity, vitality and perceptual abilities which sets up the conditions through which evolutionary progression occurs.

QUANTUM HEALING

"Blessed Bee"

My dear friend Michael Thiele says, "Altruism is one of the Bien's deepest life gestures." I love that. It matches completely my experience of the bees.

When I spoke with the bees about their medicine, they offered to share a wondrous healing method with humankind. They are exceedingly generous, full of good will, happy to share this process that supports human health. I hope you use it with reverence and respect, in the manner they describe. They first showed me an image of many bees opening the ribs of their hive-body to expose their heart, giving us trusting entry.

As a Unity, the hive is both body and being. Used erroneously, this method can cause them great harm so please, if you do this, be of the utmost integrity in your actions.

I have benefited from this prayerful healing system for some time. I have also used it with others who have health issues. A

247

good friend has been significantly helped by this. Her nervous system and organs had been damaged by a poisonous tropical spider bite four years earlier. She was so ill from the ongoing neurotoxic aftereffects and organ damage, she wondered if she'd survive.

In this stage of damage she suffered from dizziness, pain, headaches, organ pain and visual disturbances. After engaging in this healing process for half an hour, she said her symptoms were greatly reduced and successive work with the bees has taken her in a very positive direction. Over time, she has incorporated this method into her daily routine with many beneficial results.

There are three aspects to this process: prayer, sound and scent. All three can be practiced at the entrance door to any hive. If you have bees, or can find a beekeeper who will allow you to sit quietly near a hive, you may do this process right next to the hive in the warm months of the year. If being in the company of bees is not practical, or it is the cold months of winter, the bees offer another way to unite the three aspects of this healing in your own home.

Note: The resource section at the end of the book tells where you can order CDs, downloadable recordings of the sound of a thriving beehive, and fragrant healing propolis.

In Our Own Words

*[With Jacqueline's added instructions]

We tell you of a way that bees can heal humans. Enter into prayer with us as we offer the gifts of scent and sound. To partake of our medicine, do this in an atmosphere that recognizes the gift, and with reverence. In this manner we of the bee kingdom offer humans a template to create a temple of Unity.

In our healing, we offer a multidimensional path to open your mind and body to healing and your heart to love. We offer humankind a way to evolve to a place of harmony and supportive community in our shared environment on earth. In this process we have created medicine that is a healing balm for your bodies and a process that engages our souls in evolutionary progress.

Prayer

First there is prayer. Ask for healing. When you come in prayer, you open yourself into a state of grace. Let generosity flow from your heart. Come with love. Share with generosity.

This process is an exchange, not a taking. Transformation and evolution take place in the arms of joy, generosity, compassion, kindness, love. These grace states elevate our being, opening and making available the healing and evolutionary access points.

*Sit quietly by the side of a busy, thriving hive (don't block the flight path by sitting in front). If the bees continue their activities with little regard for your presence, consider yourself accepted and welcomed.

If sitting by a hive is not possible or the bees have withdrawn into the hive for the cold months, find a place in your home or yard where you can sit quietly and bring yourself into reflective, open mind space. Bring your heart in fullness as a gift. We must not simply take from them. Create a heartfelt energetic meeting with love and joy freely given. Open yourself in a prayerful and contemplative manner. Grace comes in many forms such as gratitude, peace, love, joy, inspiration, beauty, and more. Let the feeling fill your body. Take time to immerse yourself. Do not chase it. Allow it to come into you.

Sound

Listen to the sound we make. Let it fill you and bring you into our healing space.

*Bring your awareness to the sound of the hive. If you cannot sit at the side of a beehive, listen to a recording of a healthy hive through headphones. Immerse yourself in the sound.

Propolis Air

Our hive air is filled with the healing elements of the propolis. Propolis is medicine. It has the ability to go into every cell and bring healing, especially when it is airborne. It can be ingested, but it is even more powerful airborne. The propolis vapors contained in the air go directly into the blood. This stimulates an energetic state that contributes to our healing and our evolution. This can alter, repair and build anew our DNA. This is not about sniffing bee air; it is a sacred time to be present in generosity with love, and out of that comes joy, the communion of our sharing.

Propolis contains the building blocks that strengthen cells, promote healing, and bring about an evolution by communicating new information to our cells. Evolutionary medicine addresses damaged cells and heals them. All the components are present. The different combinations within propolis and within the hive are tapped.

*If you are sitting by a hive, simply breathe. In warm weather, the air around a hive is infused with the scents of honey, propolis, and the bees themselves. Just as you focused your attention on the sound, now put it gently on your sense of scent. To work outside, the weather must be warm. Cold air is not infused with scent, and in cooler months the bees will have withdrawn into the hive where they put all their energy into keeping themselves and their brood at a precise temperature. The inside hive air is meant for the bees and must be respected. Disrupting this balance can do great harm to the bees, so please follow these directions precisely.

The home process is simple. Put a thumbnail-size ball of propolis in a small covered glass jar or other confined air space. This allows the scents to accumulate and magnify their purpose. Leave the glass covered for a few hours before you begin. Let the room be warm enough that the propolis releases its healing inside the jar. Propolis is best taken into the body by inhalation where it rapidly goes into the blood and into the nervous system. Remove the lid and breathe the propolized air slowly until the breath is full.

The directions are the same for both situations, near a hive or in your home. Gently hold your breath until the scent fully absorbs into your body. Continue on, breathing the scented, infused air. Breathe deeply but normally (don't hyperventilate) for at least ten minutes and up to thirty minutes.

The scents are keys that fit into matched locks. Once matched and filled with a key, the lock opens. Stay in a receptive and meditative state while breathing the air into you. This way of healing may look simple and small but it is very powerful.

Here, the alchemical combination:
- Propolized air

- Harmonized sound

- Bringing oneself to be fully present in healing

- Knowing how to bring forth Unity

- Being in the grace states of love, generosity and joy

- Having the courage to advance in gratitude and with respect for all life.

Hive air also contains our exhalation, each little bee releasing what came before. Thus our healing moves us ever forward in the loop of time, one of the many possibilities we lay our experiences upon. Through our breath we are placed within this moment and all this moment offers us for growth. As we breathe in, we take in information about our environment, our relationships with all around us. What we find either nourishes or depletes us. Through our breath we continually strengthen our bonds to that which we imagine — to stress, fear and worry, or to love, joy and kindness. Each breath in, each breath out.

The breath in informs us of the world we dwell in. The breath out is our response to that world.

Thus it is the same with bees and humans. When we are stressed or worried, we fill the air around us with that concern, and healing may be difficult. To heal ourselves we may choose differently. What is introduced into our being has the ability to harm or heal. Our breath, such a simple act, brings us to each moment wherein we imprint that choice.

We are, after all, God's own question seeking an answer. What choice will we make and how will we live with that? Whether we are in communal group thought or the thought that comes alone, we carry forward our experience and responses to what we know.

To maintain our healthy state, we seek a clean environment. We work at the door to guard our perimeter to keep our home free of that which causes concern. If something slips in, we do our best to isolate it, encapsulate it even, so that a threat to our health moves from the interior (our home) to the exterior and thus inaccessible to our home.

Hive air moves freely in and around us. Our individual and shared responses to the air strengthen or weaken us. With each individual and collective breath we confirm our response. By that we live or die.

In the healthy hive, the air is capable of dismantling attacks and preserving health. We become strong in each moment and capable of doing our good work. Even in the presence of that which can cause disease, what we have built in our home with our medicine allows us to flourish.

Look what you surround yourself with. See what you bring into your home and ask if this brings you peace or does it cause you harm, even a little? If it does, clean it out. Once your home is secure and supports your health, you can enter into the larger environment with the wisdom to do the same outside.

Your breath brings you daily strength.

The world comes into you, mingles with your body and your thoughts, and you exhale air that expresses the being that you are.

If love circulates in your being, that which you speak and feel will come out of you. Even if what you bear is difficult, the peace you carry within will also carry into the wide world. Thus all your actions are informed by love and you become an instrument of peace and kindness.

Look within your own home. Build kindness into your relationships and care for the environment as if it was the interior of your own home, your own body. Your home, then, becomes powerfully supportive medicine that heals your weakness, gives you strength and leads you to create that which is beautiful.

VISIONARY BEES

"Realms of Infinite Possibility"

This chapter came to me while on a writing residency at Hedgebrook. Early that morning I had been wondering about possibilities. With that on my mind, I spent the morning thinking about the vast number of situations I'd hoped for in my life — like this residency — and the good luck of having so many come true. I was reviewing the sequence of coincidences and events that had led me to Hedgebrook, describing to myself each step that had to occur before the next to keep opening doors until I eventually arrived here, standing in the forest on a spring morning on Whidbey Island.

A lot. That was the answer I came up with. Some necessary steps were easy to connect, like submitting my application. Some of them seemed more random, like when my sister in southern California read an article about a writers' retreat in Washington state and suggested I inquire about it from my old home in Massachusetts. The prospect of getting a writing grant seemed pretty far-fetched and I wondered if I should bother. The most critical step was me, questioning the possibility of getting accepted and resolving to try. I could have easily decided it was too hard or too much effort and the story would have stopped there. But then it all fell together and each thought and every small action (do I have enough stamps to mail my manuscript?) was answered with a yes.

I pondered other serendipitous situations that had unexpected and positive results, like the summer after college when I rented a tiny cabin on Martha's Vineyard and took my first job teaching. My childhood home had been on a pond, and each night I fell asleep to the comforting sound of a frog chorus. One day while sitting outside the cabin I decided to dig a hole in the side yard, sink a tub in it and make a little pond with the hope frogs would find it. I borrowed a shovel and started digging. A few feet down I hit a big rock and I couldn't find the edge of it. I scraped back the dirt from the two-foot deep hole I had dug and saw white enamel. I was digging out dirt from inside a sunken tub, just where I'd imagined one should go! I finished digging, put rocks and plants in the tub and within a week frogs found it and began singing the song I'd longed to hear.

With all that on my mind, I asked the bees what I thought was a non-bee question: How does this all work? Here's how they answered.

The Overlighting Being

The quantum field is the envelope of God's thought. The field is permeable and easily accessible. It is the realm of possibility, the place of imagining. The quark comes into existence with thought as we create ideas. Multiple versions easily occur as we come to agreement on which of them to follow.

In this realm of all possibility, diamonds may be born out of a thought of coal. What we imagine can be so.

These ideas bubble up within the medium, hovering in the matrix. The conceptual framework of thought exists in many dimensions. As such, the image of bees popping through the field into a relationship with man was just such an event.

One of the many ways to create a quark is to imagine the future (though one could just as easily imagine the past). No need to get caught in illusory constructs of time; it's all within the realm of possibility and what is not, soon is, though challenging to talk of the field outside the hem of time. That is only the construct of a language formed of past - present - future that wraps our thoughts. All is possible. Ideas based in time are as simple as Mobius strips.

Our development has come through understanding mechanics and cause and effect, a wonderful evolutionary step, delightful to the intellect. We create a quark and place it into the field where it bakes like a pie.

Time * Space * Emotion (fuel) * Possibility

Bees move easily in and through the quantum field. Location is a good example. A bee scouts a new home as the swarm rests on a branch. When she finds a possible home, she enters it. As she moves through the enclosure, her mind overlaps the template of 'hive' onto the space — projecting it like a movie, fully inhabited — how the colony's home will fit and function here. She draws the image from the field where the template already exists. As she does this, the projection simultaneously appears in the consciousness of the swarm, who is in a different location. Thus the swarm knows the suitability of the site before the rest of them have even visited it.

The waggle dance is a street address; the way a bee with an exciting discovery can put emotion into the find and help make it so. Emotion fuels the manifestation. The dance sends creative energy to the quark and helps it manifest.

Though the dance may seem the practical way of communicating a location, and in part it does do that, the emotion and excitement of the discovery helps create its successful transition to being. The dance is the fuel — as all hope, desire, loss, joy, anticipation, frustration, exuberance, worry, doubt, delight, and other emotions are. Each has a distinct fuel that aids manifestation. Love is fuel but different from these other emotions in that it is indeed part of the blanket upon and through that which calls into being occurs. Love is the medium upon which all ideas birth. The quantum field itself is love. From here springs all possibility and our ever-emerging advancing evolution.

THE SONG
OF
INCREASE

VII

The Song of Sharing

Bees have been serving us for thousands of years. Now they are in desperate need of our help. Whether you have hives of your own or just care about bees and would like to be as bee- friendly as your circumstances allow, everyone can help bees in some way. If you have the room and the inclination, keeping bees can be immensely rewarding when done with respect, love, and kindness. It is my sincere hope that these lessons from the bees will influence many beekeepers to use their principles and become bee-centric beekeepers.

If you have a yard, or even a small balcony, you can plant bee-friendly forage for your own and neighborhood bees. If you aren't prepared to care for honeybees, perhaps you would like to offer a beekeeper space for a hive or two or ten on your land. I know many beekeepers who would like to have more hives than their land can sustain, and are always looking for new sites for new hives. This way, you can enjoy bees and leave the keeping to someone more knowledgeable.

You can provide a friendly water source for bees. In dry weather, the bee colony sends groups of bees to carry back water to drink and to keep the proper humidity in the brood chamber. My favorite bee watering stations are birdbaths, but you do need to modify them for bees. Make a mound of stones, gravel, moss, and wood pieces in the water so bees can safely walk to the water's edge without falling in. Butterflies will drink from these safe perches, too. My friends Robin and Jody build the most beautiful bee watering stations by filling concrete birdbaths with crystals and moss. Place the birdbath in the shade so the sun doesn't evaporate it, and make part of your morning routine a pleasant walk to the bee watering station to replenish it. You'll be surprised how much life will center itself on this. Be creative!

Perhaps you would like a hive of your own. There are beekeeping groups in just about every community. Look for one that practices natural and treatment-free beekeeping. If you have hives, you may want to learn more bee-friendly practices so you can be an even better friend and guardian to your bees. If you already have bees, join others who are committed to bee-centric beekeeping and support each other in learning best how to do this. My key questions whenever I am about to do most anything with my bees is, "Are my actions in service to the Bien?" I ask that so I seriously look at how my decisions affect the singular hive I'm standing next to and also the Bien of the world.

Can you write? Send a good letter or email to your government representatives and let them know that you support (with your dollars and your vote) bee-friendly legislation. Let pesticide companies know that you will not purchase anything they make that harms bees. Talk to your friends about bees and what you have learned about them. Donate to The Xerces Society and other organizations that work to keep the world friendly to bees.

Eat organic and non-GMO foods. Gene-modified foods are designed to be resistant to pesticides and poisons that are harmful to bees and other life. When GMO fields are sprayed with poisons and planted with chemically treated seeds, much of the vital life force in the area dies. Please don't support this industry. Organic practices support the growth and interdependency of the land and its inhabitants — a far wiser way to care for the earth.

The bees say honey is food made in prayer. I am convinced honey truly is spiritual food. Honeybees are created by the hand of God, and I believe in them and their mission. I feel blessed when I have a spoonful of honey in me.

I'd love to see more beekeepers questioning the wisdom of conventional beekeeping methods and moving to bee-centric, clean, treatment-free systems. It starts with us. To build more awareness of these ways, ask the beekeepers at your local farmers market how they care for their bees, and let them know there are alternatives available. I do this frequently so I can suggest bee-friendly ideas with beekeepers who didn't know there were alternatives. Have a look at our resource section for enlightened groups.

Most of all, you who are beekeepers can take a stand for all the bees you meet. Raise the healthiest bees possible, free of poisons and deeply engaged in their local region. If you must buy bees, buy them from local sources so they are familiar with your weather and vegetation, and hold within them solutions to regional health issues. Be in service to Mother Nature, and provide the healthiest environment you can so the Bien may grow and develop in accord with its own wisdom.

PLANTING FOR BEES

"Anchoring Light in the Ground"

In early spring I set myself to gardening. It is still cold in March in my part of the world, but already violets, primroses, daffodils, and cherry trees are blooming. They come fast on the heels of the cold hardy snowdrops, hyacinths, and pussy willows. Even though the days are nowhere near balmy, if the sun peeks out, the bees fly out seeking early nectars and pollens.

Bees always surprise me with their commitment. If it's sunny and marginally warm — even on days I reach for my hat and gloves — they will be out harvesting from the blooms. On gray days, if the sun reaches their front porch, and the weather breaks for as little as fifteen minutes, I see them dash outside. They measure time by whether they have long enough to gather a few pollen specks and a tiny drip of nectar before sprinting back to the warmth of the hive. If it is, they go.

Bees need plenty of flowers and the closer they are to home, the more time they can spend gathering pollen and nectar and the less time flying. Whether you keep bees or just want to help bees, plant flowers! If you are going to plant flowers, here are a few guidelines to help you choose what, when, and where to plant for bees and other pollinators.

COLORS

Bees are more attracted to certain colors than others. Bees prefer, in this order of priority, purple, violet, blue, blue-green, yellow, and white. Keep those colors in mind when you are planting your bee garden. Bees have a hard time seeing red (it looks like black to them) though they can see orange. Many colors visible to bees are not in the same spectrum as colors for humans, which is difficult for us to imagine. Bees perceive more through the ultraviolet (UV) spectrum, which also helps them see where the nectar and pollen are hidden.

PLANT CLOSE TOGETHER

Bees like to forage in areas that have plenty of flowers, especially similar flowers, so group your plants into a more closely planted space rather than separating them into distant areas. Sometimes people tell me, with great sadness, that no bees visit their garden. I have a few ideas about what may be causing that, and a solution for each.

1) If your neighbors don't have blooming flower gardens nearby, it may not be worth the bee's time to fly so far for one garden stopover. You will need to attract them by making your place a spectacular pollinator kingdom.

2) The flowers you have planted may be scattered too far apart from each other and would take too long to pollinate. Make your plantings more cohesive.

3) You may live in a neighborhood where people use bee-killing chemicals. Read on.

NO POISONS

If your neighbors are using bee-killing poisons, it will be difficult to attract bees and keep them alive. They will travel all through the neighborhood and sooner or later, they will find the poison. My experience is that most people are quite unaware that our laws still allow bee-killing chemicals on the market. Many people still believe if they can buy it off the shelf, it is safe enough. Educate your neighbors about moving to treatment-free gardening, or at least to organic methods so bees can survive.

I have been working for years to persuade neighbors who use toxic poisons to shift over to organics. It doesn't usually happen overnight, but with gentle persistence and friendly help, it can be done. I was very worried about a neighbor who sprayed toxic chemicals on her fruit trees because I have had colonies die from pesticides in the past.

A pesticide kill is an egregious crime against Nature. Over the years I have lost hives three different times from someone using pesticides nearby. Because bees travel up to two miles away in their pollination duties, I would be hard pressed to figure out who sprayed that day. I do, however, know that it happened the same way each time.

The about-to-become-a-bee-killer person wakes up on a Saturday morning and notices his peach tree is blooming. He suddenly remembers he forgot to spray the tree when it was still in bud. He ignores the directions that say never to spray when a tree is blooming because that's when pollinators visit. He disregards that the directions say to spray only on windless days so the poison doesn't travel far, and that it's best to spray at dawn or dusk when the bees are not out. To the person spraying, it's midday on a weekend and he's got time right now, better late than never. Not noticing my bees in the tree doing their pollinating job, he sprays the tree and the bees unknowingly bring that poison home to the hive.

Bees touch each other numerous times through the day. One study said that if a handful of bees come home sticky with poison, that within twenty-four hours every bee in the hive will have touched a bee who touched a bee and the entire colony will be poisoned. Each time one of my colonies got poisoned, it took one or two days for them to die a slow, painful death. I have watched with tears in my eyes as they succumbed to the terrible neurotoxic effects and there is no doubt in my mind they suffer badly. There is nothing I can do to help. I can't wash them off. Once the poison is in them, they are on the death path. Bee-killing chemicals ought to be outlawed.

At first my neighbor was not open to changing how she gardened and that is as far as I got each year. I like her plenty, we just disagreed on this. Eventually I asked her if she'd at least let me know the day before she sprayed so I could keep my bees inside. This year she called me the night before (a small success!) and I thanked her for her consideration.

Then I asked if she'd tell me the name of the pesticide she'd be spraying. I went online and found out what it did, then called back and asked if I could buy her the organic version. I even offered to pay for it because the alternative — many dead hives — was so horrific. She agreed (a huge success!) so I drove to the nearest nursery that stocked the organic version and bought it for her. She used it that night and my bees survived.

Keep in mind that poison is poison. Even though something is organic, it doesn't always mean it is bee-friendly. I helped my neighbor read the directions and encouraged her to spray on a windless day toward evening when my bees were all safely in their hives. If someone is going to spray toxic chemicals on their fruit tree or garden vegetables, it's important this not be done when the plants or tree are in flower because that is when bees are most likely to visit.

I encourage people to use their common sense and examine why we'd want to eat food that has poisons on it in the first place. We can start making these changes by becoming sensitive to our own health and avoiding poisons. From there we can extend that attitude out to bees and bee health. Poisons kill, that's their purpose. How can that not have an effect on our own bodies, our children's health and the longevity of honeybees?

SINGLE PETALS RULE

Bees don't want to spend valuable time figuring out where the pollen is on a multi- petalled flower. Single-petalled flowers, like cosmos and sunflowers, have pollen that is easier to find than complicated chrysanthemums and tight-petalled roses. Stay simple.

Flowers need to have nectar and pollen openings that match the bee's tongue length and body size. The throat of monardia (bee balm) fits a bumblebee perfectly but is too long and narrow for the honeybee's tongue. Squash flowers are wide inside and a riot of joy for honeybees. I've seen as many as five bees inside an open squash flower at once, all of them covered head-to-toe with golden pollen.

I dug out a clump of flashy asian lilies when I realized none of my bees had any interest in them. Our honeybees are originally

European honeybees and they do not have a historical memory for flowers from an unknown continent. I planted bee-friendly rudbeckia (brown-eyed susans) there instead, and they're well-visited by bees.

CLUMPS

When a bee visits a garden, she is on a mission to gather pollen from one kind of flower. That is what makes pollination work! If your sage, mint, lavender and wisteria are all blooming at once, one group of foragers will focus on lavender while another visits all the wisteria. Rather than planting lavender here and there, bees are happier and can be more efficient if you put all your lavender plants in one close area.

BLOOMS IN EVERY SEASON

In the Pacific northwest, most of our blooms happen in spring. Everything flowers until the drier weather of midsummer comes. Less and less comes into bloom as we move toward fall. I want my bees to be busy right to the tail end of October so I plant lots of summer and fall blooming plants like joe-pye weed, goldenrod, asters, salvia, and autumn joy sedum. Wherever you are, be sure your garden has a few things in bloom through all the seasons your bees are in the garden, and plant extra in the slower seasons. Don't let the bees run out of food.

BEE MEDICINE

Plant flowering herbs! Even a tiny bit of room on an apartment patio deck can help the bees. Not only do bees collect nectar and pollen from herbs, they also gather essential oils from flowers.

These essential oils are added to wax and propolis to create the air-infused medicine the bees breathe. Lavender, borage, catnip, fennel, all the mints, rosemary, sage, and thyme are particularly good for bees.

In Our Own Words

What makes bees happy? The shape of scents, the sweet of nectars, the sun's prismatic light, our cumulative joy.

Flowers are an embodiment of light anchored in the ground. The plant has a relationship with the Sun and the light that raises it up and toward the sky and Sun. We go out and collect pollen, which is materialized light, and bring it back to the hive.

Each grain of pollen is an anthology of information about local flora and the mineral terrain. We develop and grow on a diet of the landscape. Each mineral and plant speaks to us in our nascent form, describing in a wordless language the pitch and flow of the flora.

Later, after we are born and flying, we experience the jubilant excitement of discovering these flavor-scents in the land around the hive. We understand our place through these familiar reacquaintances with what we first knew and became kin with in the cells of the nursery.

OPENING THE HIVE

"Let Your Heart Precede You"

One way beekeepers can help their bees is simply to open the hive less often. New beekeepers especially seem to have a burning need to get into their hives and see what is going on. While it is an education to peek inside, it is always a setback — sometimes a major one — for the bees.

Bees work hard to create a protective, healing seal in their hive space and to keep a specific and precise temperature for the brood. It takes the bees about a day-and-a-half to restore the balance in their hive after it has been opened and inspected. Still, there are times when hives must be opened to check on the health of the hive, add or remove a hive box, or gather honey.

When I need to open my hives, I am always conscious of where I am standing, what the weather is doing and how the bees are feeling that day. Standing in the flight path, opening a hive in cold weather and dangerously chilling your bees, or not respecting warning buzzes or bumps from guard bees are recipes for certain disaster.

I open my hives on warm days when the bees let me know they are not dealing with their own stresses that day. I always move very slowly and quietly which brings calmness to the bees and to me, too. Most important: I bring loving and caring intent into my actions, and purposely pour love into the open hive. I cannot over-state how important intention and loving-kindness are to the bees. They speak of it often.

In Our Own Words

Breaking the propolis seal opens the hive to outer influences that are hard to control.

Some human participation is okay. Bees are, after all, do-mesticated, but this must be done with presence and attention to the sacredness of our hive. Open our home with a ritual, full of prayer and love as you come into communion with us.

Many beekeepers open a hive with focus on the hive but little genuine and heartfelt interaction. We are not simply a science project. When you open our hive respectfully, open yourself too, to being blessed. Ask to open and wait for the answer. Open and pause. Let your heart precede you. Feel the emanation from the hive and let it enter you. Move slowly and gently. You are in our home, a holy place.

Learn the difference between hovering, observing, and be-ing present. The energy moves between us. Open your heart to feel the presence of our family, to our hive and to this expanding sphere of presence between us. At the point where familiarity dwells, let us embrace you, too.

Daily give your blessing to the bees who you are partnered with. We do know it, and it strengthens us to be blessed, as it does us all.

THE WHOLE & HOLY LIFE

"Seeking the Evolution of All Beings"

Co-evolution thrills me because I see the interrelatedness of life and how we merry make our way into the future.

When my husband and I bought our land, we entered into a partnership with the farm that is much like a marriage. We believe the farm is a cohesive, living entity and far more than the plants and soil, animals and insects that live in and upon it. Often we tend to think of that as resources and within that thought come questions about how we can use those resources, often for profit and not always with the land's best interest at heart. When my husband and I plan what next to do here, we include the farm's perspective in all our decisions. Quite often the farm's opinion outweighs our own, and we are bettered by it.

By our fourth year on the farm, we had chickens, honeybees and a small garden. By no means, was the farm established at that point. What we had was the same as many city dwellers. Then I began dreaming of cows — cows in lush green pastures, milking cows, cows mooing to us — all things I'd never dreamed about before. It was an outright peculiarity, and I took it to mean the farm was asking for cows. Neither of us had been inclined to get a cow, but the farm wanted cows and presented us with many reasons why a cow would be good for us: improving the land and our health; creating a loving relationship with a new animal; helping us develop commitment and deepen friendships within our community.

That seemed like a tall order, but we went ahead and bought a lovely cow who became mother to many. Over time, we sold or traded the heifers to our neighbors. After a few years, we called all the neighborhood cows together and built a community herd with shared pastures and chores. I would not have imagined such a thing if we hadn't paid attention to those incongruous thoughts. The harmony and satisfaction that comes of living in agreement with our land and farm brings us great joy. On a personal level, I want to live my life in such a way that the presence of God is all around me, as I imagine it is when these mundane and miraculous moments occur. As such, I desire to witness and support that which is highest in each person I know, holding that someday I may be a better reflection of God to know the world through me. In the meantime, I seek to build Life Force around us in every way I can. Our farm is a good place to do this.

Wherever you live is a good place to do this. Each of us can become a contributing part of a Bien: Somewhere near to where you live, a colony may be tending your home, your breath, your sunlight, flowers and nature spirits. The bees who give attention to your garden may be from your own hives, or perhaps wild bees up in a wooded, high bower have enfolded you into their universe. You are part of a Bien, maybe more than one. You are already within the Unity, and you have a gift to contribute. Step forward, and give your love and your joy to this glorious task.

The Overlighting Being

Each piece of land dwelled upon bespeaks the balance of all the beings present upon that land, and of the multiple dimensions of the land's life beings. This is written as a code, a tally of the balance (or unbalance) that place bears. Imagine the code suspended over the land, like a street address, able to be read by anyone cognizant of these forces. Thus it sits, an open-ended equation that can be added to, subtracted from, multiplied with, or separated by division. Certain combinations open new possibilities, acting by their presence as harbingers of possible development.

As humans, a contribution is made by developing the higher self. The community present on the land is influenced by the emotional tones carried in each human. These powerful singings help or hinder the development and expression of all the beings also present. Humans who dwell in strongly negative energies are capable of undoing eons of expression and bring the land presence to doldrums wherein forward advancement comes to pause. Such human action may not seem significant on its own but in party to all the presences, it can influence or stall the co-evolution.

Nature seeks the evolution of all beings in their own turn, and indeed the co-evolution wherein all are party to each other's blended progress.

In such a way, bees and man co-evolve. But while humans may well 'keep bees,' the kingdom of bees indeed longs to sing the song of shared awareness, of our mutual caring for one another. Bees enrich and harmonize the environment each day, helping Nature in so many ways, to fulfill the evolutionary directive.

When man comes present, knowing of these relationships, the code activates. When intellect outweighs knowledge of the relationships, man falters in his development and introduces a di-

vision because he separates his actions into what benefits him alone. Progress halts because the code is unbalanced, and needed components and energies are deprived of their valences.

To evolve in the current time, love needs to be present. When working with the bees and with each other, ask your hands and your hearts to be gentle, let your mind be guided to actions that fulfill the purpose of bees in the world, not for shortsighted solutions or harvests that unbalance the colony's needs. Learn to respect the sanctity of the bond. Use that knowledge to become kinder, more compassionate, and walk forward into the future, all of us together, emanating and enveloped in our shared love and awakening.

THE SONG
OF
INCREASE

EPILOGUE

"Bee Sleepover"

And now we reach the end of this book. I hope through reading this, you are more inclined to see the world as a bee would, and care for this earth so all may live and flourish.

Alas, most people still are afraid of bees. Many of those people have little or no experience with bees on which to base their fearfulness. Why are so many people scared? The media doesn't tell us that bees are inclined to be good-natured. News programs rarely distinguish between hornets, yellow jackets and wasps. All are called "bees." Until recently, bees didn't generally make news because bees are very quiet and beekeeping has generally been a peaceful hobby that many people take to in retirement. Then came alarming stories of killer bees aggressively attacking people and animals, terrifying tales of giant Asian wasps with nasty dispositions. When I work the bee booth at the county fair, people often timidly ask how to protect themselves from bee attacks.

I tell them my experience, how I am around bees a lot and I rarely have a moment of concern. When working with the hive, bee gloves would protect my hands from stings but they are clunky. I prefer bare hands and that works well for most tasks. If the bees are uneasy (and sometimes they are), I take that as a signal to go slower or maybe come back another day.

This afternoon, I found a bee caught against the garage window and invited her onto my finger so I could walk her outside, where she flew off. When I find a bee in the house (open honey container + open window = bees in the kitchen), I gently carry her outdoors. I want to handle bees so they are reassured of their safety and well-being.

Away from the hive, a single honeybee is an adventurer, an intrepid explorer for the daytime hours. Alone she cannot survive. If a foraging bee gets lost or trapped during her travel and is stuck somewhere overnight, most likely she will be dead by morning.

If we leave our south-facing garage door open, I check the west windows late in the day for errant bees. The bees who live in our north hives often forage in the southeast field and if they try to take a shortcut back through our garage, they get caught against the west windows that don't open. You would imagine these bees would eventually figure out that they cannot get through the window and go back out through the door, but that isn't what happens. Curiously, I also find butterflies, moths, crane flies, mason bees and ladybugs in the windows, and they nearly always find their way out quickly. Only the honeybees get caught there and die.

Each bee has a tiny speck of magnetic oxide nanoparticles concentrated in her antennae and abdomen that guide her home. When a bee flies up against that west-facing window, she is absolutely sure home is in that direction. She knows that route will take her home if she can just get past the window. She will continue trying to go that way until she exhausts herself and dies. A honeybee cannot override her sense of direction and that's why I need to check those windows and move any stuck bees.

Sometimes after dark I find a bee in the house, buzzing against a light fixture. A bee can't fly at night without the sun to help her navigate home. If I release her outside, she will simply get lost and most likely die. Because we have multiple hives here, I don't know which one is her home so it is impossible to deliver her to the correct hive. I have tried putting these evening bees on the front step of the nearest hive and sometimes that works — the little girl slips right inside — but just as many times the guard bees come out and give the stranger a rough once-over. When that happens I suddenly have a lost and scared bee on my hands. Alas, what to do?

I tried putting a dish with a dab of honey on my counter, then putting a glass jar over the dish. That kept her confined until morning, but I noticed she often spent a stressful evening buzzing against the glass trying to get out. When I thought of her natural environment, I came up with something different: the bee sleepover jar.

I placed two small chunks of empty comb and a tiny smidge of highly scented propolis inside a pint glass jar. I pressed the edges of the wax so it adhered to the sides, leaving room between the combs so it appears similar to the inside of a hive. Using a toothpick, I filled one cell near the top with honey and I put a single tiny drop of water in another cell — a pinhead size drop. Then I poked tiny airholes into the metal cap or I used the screened top of a sprouting jar cover.

When I find a bee after dark, I introduce her to her overnight honeybee guest room. I tell her I have a safe place for her to rest until morning. Using my finger, I gently place her inside the jar and let her walk onto the comb, then I screw the ventilated top on and put her in a darkened room. Sometimes I find two or three bees out for the evening, buzzing about in my kitchen. I put them together, and they all have a friendly sleepover in the comb jar.

Bees are used to being on comb. These foragers are stressed about being out after dark, so I want to recreate a hive-ish place to give them a sense of familiarity about where they are, with their natural scents of wax comb, fragrant propolis, sweet honey, and water all nearby.

Once I have the bees safely settled in for the evening, I WRITE MYSELF A NOTE to remind me in the morning that my little lost bees are in the parlor. I write the note because I have twice awakened and gone about my day, forgetting the bee jar until later. By then, their time apart from the colony was too long, and the bees had died. Now I tape notes on the bathroom mirror, my office desk and the kitchen table.

After the sun comes up, I peek at the sleepover bees in the jar and nearly always they are just fine. Once they start moving around, I walk up the path to the bee yard and open the jar. They immediately fly home.

You, too, can create a small bee bed-and-breakfast with a pint jar and some pieces of comb. Each evening at dusk I like to make the rounds and check that no bees are caught in the greenhouse, garage windows, in the kitchen. This attentiveness to bees around you — noticing stragglers in your midst — is a simple and wonderful meditative practice on awareness and kindness, benefiting you and the bees.

Does it matter that one little bee makes it through the night?

I believe it does. Being kind to one bee, when it likely won't make much difference to the hive or even the bee community, is a good thing for us humans to do. Maybe the world won't change because I saved a bee. But, too often, the callousness of my inattention denies me the opportunity to develop benevolence. No being is inconsequential; every life matters. When we treat all beings as deserving of our consideration, even a little bee can assist us in our task of becoming gentler, more thoughtful, more human.

THE SONG
OF
INCREASE

RESOURCES

Below is a fine collection bee books, DVDs, websites, and articles to deepen your knowledge and appreciation of the honeybee.

BOOKS

Toward Saving the Honeybee, Gunther Hauk

Queen of the Sun, anthology compiled by Taggart Siegel and Jon Betz

The Buzz About Bees, Jurgen Tautz

Bees and Honey: From Flower to Jar, Michael Weiler

The Bee-Friendly Beekeeper: A Sustainable Approach, David Heaf

Bee Propolis: Natural Healing from the Hive, James Fearnley

The Global Hive, Horst Kornberger

DVDS & VIDEOS

Alternative Beekeeping Using the Top Bar Hive and The Bee Guardian Methods, Corwin Bell at www.BackyardHive.com (Every beekeeper should have this video.)

Queen of the Sun, Award winning and visually stunning documentary about bees and beekeepers who are working in bee-centric ways.

Videos by Michael Thiele, always engaging bees with respect, on www.GaiaBees.com

Audio CD and files of colonies singing "The Song of Increase" and other fascinating states of being in the hive. Sound by Robin Wise. This is a good audiofile to listen to during a bee medicine session. www.SpiritBee.com

BEE STUFF

Mickelberry Gardens www.mickelberrygardens.com
Organic and treatment-free gifts from the hive including propolis for healing. (See the Quantum Healing chapter.)

HELPFUL ORGANIZATIONS & INTERNET GROUPS

The Xerces Society, www.xerces.org Every beekeeper ought to support this organization. They do vital work to protect bees and other pollinators.

The Organic Beekeepers Group — a treatment-free internet group who meets annually for a wide- ranging educational conference organicbeekeepers-subscribe@yahoogroups.com

Warre Beekeeping — David Heaf and other helpful beekeepers who use Warre hives
https://uk.groups.yahoo.com/neo/groups/warrebeekeeping/info

Phil Chandler's Biobees, www.biobees.com

The Melissa Garden, www.themelissagarden.com

ARTICLES

Quantum Honeybees, Writer Adam Frank describes mathematician Barbara Shipman's discoveries about the quantum aspects of the bee waggle dance at: www.discovermagazine.com/1997/nov/quantumhoneybees1263

Lilipoh magazine, Summer 2008, issue 52, vol. 13. Many fine articles on relating to honeybees in a more sensitive manner, especially "Honoring the Bien," by Michael Thiele.
www.lilipoh.com (Under "Past Issues")

JACQUELINE'S BEE NEWSLETTER & WEBSITE

www.SpiritBee.com

Jacqueline invites you to sign up for her seasonal bee newsletter at www.SpiritBee.com

SpiritBee is where Jacqueline and Robin Wise post their work with bees, including videos, sound files, books and photos, further writings about and from the bees, and lovely hand-designed items that use their bee imagery.

THE SONG
OF
INCREASE

ACKNOWLEDGEMENTS

I thank the bees who have been incredibly generous to share this information with me. I hope I have conveyed their brilliant knowledge in a way that helps others come to love them, too. I am grateful to our farm, Friendly Haven Rise, for the wide bounty of beauty and the feeling of love that emanates from this place.

As I wrote this book, I was surrounded by intelligent, devoted people who helped me carry this vision. I thank my husband Joseph for creating the three-dimensional framework that vividly portrayed how all aspects of bee life connect with each other and provided the foundation for this idea to light upon. Also I am grateful he transcribed many of these teachings as I spoke with the bees, which allowed me to go deeper.

I thank Patti Pitcher for her early and persistent encouragement and her wisdom in all things. I thank Sara Cooper for her insightful organization, support and delightful friendship. I thank Susan Chernak McElroy for unravelling the structure of this book and making it easy for me to understand, and for coming out and staying at the farm as I wrote so I could ask a hundred questions. Her precious guidance is what turned hundreds of stray pages into a book. I will always be grateful she put her book aside and offered to help me with mine. I look forward to more collaboration in the future.

I thank Robin Wise for accompanying me on the bee journey with her photos and audiofiles to help us see and hear all that surrounds us, and for enriching my life with her astute observations and her commitment to holding bees in a sacred manner. Catherine Diaz showed up at the perfect time with editing and design suggestions. Glenna Rose gave me the most supportive proofing ever — I felt like a better person when she finished editing.

I thank my super-smart father, Charlie Entwistle, for his inspiration and advice that I should do what I love and figure out ways to make those things become my work. His generosity and love make my heart happy. My stepmom June planted the seed by publishing her book a decade ago and ever since I have wondered how I could do that.

I thank these people whose presence in the world I thoroughly enjoy: Amber Ham, Catherine Miller-Smith, my mother Jesse, Brenda Wilson, Bonnie York, Bambi Dore, my brother CW (the first person to introduce me to bees!) and Deborah Entwistle, Kay Gleason, Nathan Rausch, my beloved Aunt Ruth, Corwin Bell, Steve Storch, Debra Roberts, Michael Thiele, Dee Lusby, Brenda Calvert, BJ Schulte, Susan Tripp, Wes Burch, Summer Michaelson, Rick Sievers and special thanks to Hedgebrook, the writing retreat that offered me the gift of quiet time and place to put this book together.

ABOUT THE AUTHOR

Jacqueline Freeman is a biodynamic farmer and a pioneer in the emerging field of natural beekeeping. She is gifted in perceiving nature intelligences, particularly honeybees, and has spent many years working alongside them with an open and prayerful heart.

In 2010 the bees began communicating to her how they fulfill broader roles in the hive and in nature. They describe the matrix of their thought and imagination, and explain their intent to assist humans in their spiritual evolution.

Jacqueline teaches bee classes at her farm and honeybee sanctuary in Washington state. The documentary movie "Queen of the Sun" showed her caring work as a gentle swarm rescuer. Her bee articles appear in national magazines and in the "Queen of the Sun" book. She's been a featured speaker at national conferences for organic and treatment-free beekeepers, permaculture, sustainable agricultural and regional events. In 2013, the Dominican Republic hired her to work with rural beekeepers to help them create healthy bees through respectful and treatment-free beekeeping.

Jacqueline's website, SpiritBee.com, has beautiful photos, movies, audio-files and hive gifts, many created with Robin Wise. You are invited to read more of her bee communications and see videos of her working with her bees through the year.

Jacqueline and her husband Joseph live on their biodynamic farm in southwest Washington.

Friendly Haven Rise Press
Battle Ground, WA
www.FriendlyHaven.com/books

Printed in Great Britain
by Amazon.co.uk, Ltd.,
Marston Gate.